T0383105

African Business Finance and Development Policy

African Business Finance and Development Policy has been co-published simultaneously as *Journal of African Business,* Volume 4, Number 2 2003.

African Business Finance and Development Policy

Victor Murinde, PhD
Atsede Woldie, PhD
Editors

African Business Finance and Development Policy has been co-published simultaneously as *Journal of African Business,* Volume 4, Number 2 2003.

International Business Press
An Imprint of
The Haworth Press, Inc.
New York • London • Oxford

Published by

International Business Press®, 10 Alice Street, Binghamton, NY 13904-1580 USA

International Business Press® is an imprint of The Haworth Press, Inc., 10 Alice Street, Binghamton, NY 13904-1580 USA.

African Business Finance and Development Policy has been co-published simultaneously as *Journal of African Business,* Volume 4, Number 2 2003.

The development, preparation, and publication of this work has been undertaken with great care. However, the publisher, employees, editors, and agents of The Haworth Press and all imprints of The Haworth Press, Inc., including The Haworth Medical Press® and The Pharmaceutical Products Press®, are not responsible for any errors contained herein or for consequences that may ensue from use of materials or information contained in this work. Opinions expressed by the author(s) are not necessarily those of The Haworth Press, Inc.

Cover design by Lora Wiggins.

Library of Congress Cataloging-in-Publication Data

African business finance and development policy / Victor Murinde, Atsede Woldie, editors.
    p. cm.
    Papers presented at an international conference held at the Institute for Developmental Policy and Management, University of Manchester, England, April 2001.
    "African business finance and development policy has been co-published simultaneously as Journal of African Business, Volume 4, Number 2 2003."
    Includes bibliographical references and index.
    ISBN 0-7890-2084-X (hardcover : alk. paper) – ISBN 0-7890-2085-8 (softcover : alk. paper)
    1. Finance–Government policy–Africa–Congresses. 2. Finance–Africa–Congresses. 3. Banks and banking–Government policy–Africa–Congresses. 4. Banks and banking–Africa–Congresses. 5. Africa–Commercial policy–Congresses. 6. Africa–Economic policy–Congresses. I. Murinde, Victor. II. Woldie, Atsede.
HG187.5.A327 2003
332'.096–dc21
                                                                                    2003000049

Indexing, Abstracting & Website/Internet Coverage

This section provides you with a list of major indexing & abstracting services. That is to say, each service began covering this periodical during the year noted in the right column. Most Websites which are listed below have indicated that they will either post, disseminate, compile, archive, cite or alert their own Website users with research-based content from this work. (This list is as current as the copyright date of this publication.)

Abstracting, Website/Indexing Coverage . . . . Year When Coverage Began

- *AURSI African Urban & Regional Science Index,*
  a scholarly & research index which synthesises &
  compiles all publications on urbanization & regional
  science in Africa within the world. Published annually **1999**

- *Cambridge Scientific Abstracts (Risk Abstracts)*
  <www.csa.com> **2001**

- *CNPIEC Reference Guide: Chinese National Directory*
  of Foreign Periodicals **1999**

- *EconLit, on CD-ROM, and e-JEL* **2000**

- *Emerald Management Reviews (formerly known as*
  Anbar Management Intelligence Abstracts)
  <www.emeraldinsight.com/reviews/index.htm> **2000**

- *FINDEX <www.publist.com>* **1999**

- *FISHLIT <www.nisc.co.za>* **2000**

- *FRANCIS.INIST/CNRS <www.inist.fr>* **2000**

- *GEO Abstracts (GEO Abstracts/GEOBASE)*
  URL: http://elsevier.nl **2000**

(continued)

Special Bibliographic Notes related to special journal issues (separates) and indexing/abstracting:

- indexing/abstracting services in this list will also cover material in any "separate" that is co-published simultaneously with Haworth's special thematic journal issue or DocuSerial. Indexing/abstracting usually covers material at the article/chapter level.
- monographic co-editions are intended for either non-subscribers or libraries which intend to purchase a second copy for their circulating collections.
- monographic co-editions are reported to all jobbers/wholesalers/approval plans. The source journal is listed as the "series" to assist the prevention of duplicate purchasing in the same manner utilized for books-in-series.
- to facilitate user/access services all indexing/abstracting services are encouraged to utilize the co-indexing entry note indicated at the bottom of the first page of each article/chapter/contribution.
- this is intended to assist a library user of any reference tool (whether print, electronic, online, or CD-ROM) to locate the monographic version if the library has purchased this version but not a subscription to the source journal.
- individual articles/chapters in any Haworth publication are also available through the Haworth Document Delivery Service (HDDS).

African Business Finance and Development Policy

CONTENTS

ABOUT THE EDITORS

Victor Murinde (BA, MSc, PhD), is Professor of Development Finance and Head of Finance Group, Birmingham Business School, University of Birmingham. He is also Visiting Professor in Development Finance at the Institute for Development Policy and Management (IDPM), University of Manchester.

Lecturing experience at Makerere University, Cardiff Business School, Bradford University, Loughborough University and Manchester University. Advisory services to many international organisations, including the World Bank, the United Nations, UNCTAD, Kuwait Institute of Scientific Research, African Development Bank, and the Caribbean Development Bank, as well as many governments and private sector companies.

Professor Murinde has published over forty articles in many leading journals including the *Journal of Banking and Finance*, *Journal of International Money and Finance*, *Review of International Economics*, *Manchester School*, *Journal of Policy Modelling*, *Emerging Markets Review*, *Applied Financial Economics*, *International Journal of Theoretical and Applied Finance*, *Research in Accounting in Emerging Economies*, *World Development*, *Economic Notes and Applied Economics*. His recent research monographs include *Macroeconomic Policy Modelling for Developing Countries* (Avebury, 1993; reprinted 1995), *Development Banking and Finance* (Avebury, 1996; reprinted 1997), *Financial Sector Reform and Privatisation in Transition Economies* (Elsevier Science B.V., North Holland, 1998, edited with J. Doukas and C. Wihlborg), *Trade Regime and Economic Growth* (Ashgate Publishing Ltd, 1998; co-authored with Charles L. Chanthunya), *The Free Trade Area of the Common Market for Eastern and Southern Africa* (Ashgate Publishing Ltd, 2001) and the first ever *Handbook of International Banking* (co-edited with Andy W. Mullineux and published by Edward Elgar, 2003). Current research interests include: the microstructure of emerging financial markets; corporate finance issues surrounding capital structure and dividend policy; bank performance and risk; and flow-of-funds, financial development and poverty reduction.

Professor Murinde's research has been funded mainly by generous grants from the European Commission (EC), the UK Department for International Development (DFID), the ESRC and the Leverhulme Trust.

Atsede Woldie (DipC, PGCertME, PGDipA, BA, MsocSci, PhD), is Senior Lecturer and Course Leader for the MSc Management and International Financial System Development at the University of Glamorgan. Dr. Woldie's PhD is in Development Finance at Birmingham University, consequent upon achieving the prestigious World Bank Award for the promotion of further research in promoting economic development in emerging and developing countries.

Working experience at Ministry of Mines, Ethiopian Telecommunications, Ethiopian Wood Work Corporations, Ethiopian Management Institute, Addis Ababa, Ethiopia.

Lecturing experience at the Ethiopian Management Institute and Birmingham University. Dr. Woldie is a qualified and certified Management Educator and a member of the Staff Development Committee at the University of Glamorgan. Advisory services to private and public organisations including Welsh Development Agency and Welsh Assembly, Bute Town History and Arts Centre, Cardiff.

Dr. Woldie has published widely in the field of total quality management control of the delivery of banking services as well as small business finance in international journals. She is on the editorial board of the *Middle East Business Review Journal, Journal of African Business* and *The Journal of Indonesian Management and Accounting Research*. Dr. Woldie is a key member of groups addressing issues of economic regeneration and development in Wales.

Current research includes: financial development and poverty reduction, Islamic banking, service quality in banking, small business finance and female entrepreneurs in a transitional economy.

Introduction

Sam C. Okoroafo

There has been a longstanding interest in the contribution that finance makes to economic growth and development. In the light of the growing consensus that development policy should focus on poverty reduction, the past few years have seen a renewed concern with the design and implementation of financial policies for pro-poor growth and poverty alleviation in developing countries. This special issue of the *Journal of African Business* contains a set of seven papers on the theme of "development and business finance: policy and experience in developing countries." The papers were carefully reviewed and selected from approximately 31 papers which were presented at an international conference held at the Institute for Development Policy and Management, University of Manchester, in April 2001. The conference carefully explored a number of key policy issues by bringing together researchers and practitioners in the field of development finance, especially with respect to banking, business finance, and investment in developing countries. A number of unique topics are discussed, such as strategies for coping with a small financial system, bank licensing policies, prompt corrective action rules, quality of banking services, and revitalisation of African stock exchange. The topics cover a number of countries in Sub-Sahara Africa, including Kenya, Zambia, Nigeria, Mauritius and Zimbabwe.

First, Bossone and Honohan note that about 60 countries have small financial systems each with a total size (measured in terms of M2) of

[Haworth co-indexing entry note]: "Introduction." Okoroafo, Sam C. Co-published simultaneously in *Journal of African Business* (International Business Press, an imprint of The Haworth Press, Inc.) Vol. 4, No. 2, 2003, pp. 1-4; and: *African Business Finance and Development Policy* (eds: Victor Murinde and Atsede Woldie) International Business Press, an imprint of The Haworth Press, Inc., 2003, pp. 1-4. Single or multiple copies of this article are available for a fee from The Haworth Document Delivery Service [1-800-HAWORTH, 9:00 a.m. - 5:00 p.m. (EST). E-mail address: docdelivery@haworthpress.com].

http://www.haworthpress.com/store/product.asp?sku=J156
10.1300/J156v04n02_01

less than $1 billion. The authors believe that the size of financial system is relevant and argue that the ability of small financial systems to diversify risk and provide adequate liquidity is limited. Furthermore, it is argued that small financial systems are less competitive, incomplete and more costly to regulate and supervise. The authors examine the status in Africa and note that sub-Saharan African countries have the largest concentration of small financial systems. Some ideas are suggested on strategies that may help countries to cope with the small size of the financial system, including: foreign ownership of financial intermediaries; regional securities markets; shared regional infrastructure; open capital flows; and a common currency. Examples here include the South African Development Community (SADC) and the co-operative financial sector arrangements in the CFA Franc Zone.

Second, Maimbo examines bank-licensing policies in the period before and after the bank failures in Zambia in 1980-1994. Bank licensing policies and procedures comprise an important aspect of the development of the financial sector in many sub-Saharan African countries. Maimbo's study identifies significant deficiencies in bank licensing policies. First, the focus is on the minimum legally-required capital requirements neglecting the need for banks to raise sufficient business capital. Second, the source and existence of capital was not thoroughly investigated. Third, the Ministry of Finance had no criteria for assessing the character and experience of major shareholders and directors. Finally, there were many former senior BCCI officials that entered the banking sector through the newly-licensed banks, either as owners or managers. However, the study could not confirm its hypothesis that weaknesses in the bank licensing policies and procedures were significant contributing factors to the 1995-1997/8 bank failures. The paper calls for further research on prudential entry requirements in African economies.

Third, Brownbridge and Maimbo examine the potential benefits and feasibility of incorporating "Prompt Correction Action" (PCA) rules into banking regulation in developing countries. Regulatory forbearance is a critical weakness in prudential regulation in many developing countries. The aim of the PCA rules is to force the regulators to intervene earlier and more effectively in distressed banks. It will limit the discretion of the regulators to intervene in the affairs of distressed banks, by mandating the regulators to undertake specific interventions on a timely basis. The study also identified constraints to the effective implementation of PCA rules in developing countries, including lack of timely and accurate financial data and lack of adequate legal autonomy

from government. It is argued that, despite these constraints, the introduction of PCA rules into the banking laws of developing countries can
bring positive benefits. It is recommended that, because the law will
mandate regulatory intervention, PCA rules should improve incentives
on the regulators to act more promptly to tackle problems in distressed
banks and provide the regulators with some protection against pressure
for regulatory forbearance from politicians and bankers.

Fourth, Woldie examines the quality of banking services in Nigeria.
Service quality in banking is becoming more important in bank service
marketing. The study examines organisations' perceptions of the level
of service quality provided by Commercial Banks in Nigeria. A questionnaire survey was conducted amongst 150 small and medium-sized
firms in Nigeria. The findings of the research suggest that the key factors in selecting a particular bank are credibility, location and range of
services. The research also indicates that complicated procedures and
forms, queuing time, lack of individualized approach and absence of
new technology are some of the factors which create dissatisfaction,
and lack of co-operation between firms and banks. These results are
similar to those obtained from customers in developed countries.

Fifth, it is noted that most African countries are revitalising existing
stock markets and establishing new ones. Ngugi, Murinde and Green
investigate the response of emerging stock markets in Africa to various
reforms implemented during the revitalising process using a sample
from 10 selected African countries. The study identifies three main
types of reforms, namely the strengthening of the regulatory framework, shifts in trading system and adoption of modern trading technology, and relaxation of restrictions on the participation of foreign
investors. The main findings of the study suggest that the reforms have
been fruitful in terms of improvements in the market microstructure of
African stock exchanges.

Sixth, Manos and Clairette Ah-Hen examine the determinants of capital structure of firms in Mauritius. A model, which predicts the main
determinants of leverage, is tested on a sample of 24 firms using the
panel procedure over the period 1992-2000. The findings seem to support the pecking order theory and reject the trade-off theory of capital
structure, in the context of Mauritius.

Seventh, Mutenheri and Green report on the impact of economic reform programmes on the financing choices of Zimbabwean listed companies. Using company accounts data from 52 non-financial companies
listed on the Zimbabwe Stock Exchange, the authors note that listed
firms rely heavily on external finance, especially short-term bank fi-

nancing, whereas long-term bank loans make little contribution to financing of the corporate sector. The study also finds that an orthodox model has little explanatory power over firms' capital structure in the pre-reform period, but in the post-reform period, asset tangibility, tax rates, growth opportunities, earnings volatility and bank liquidity are all significant determinants of capital structure. The differences between the pre-reform and post-reform era suggest that the reforms did achieve a partial success in opening up the capital markets and improving the transparency of firm financing behaviour.

Coping with a Small Financial System: Policy Issues for Africa

Biagio Bossone
Patrick Honohan

SUMMARY. Does it matter that all of the sub-Saharan African countries have small financial systems? In this short paper, we review the reasons why absolute size is relevant, and consider some of the possible ways of alleviating the problems resulting from having a small financial system. One of the potential solutions is regional cooperation. This has already been tried, with a degree of success, in parts of Africa. More could be done. *[Article copies available for a fee from The Haworth Document Delivery Service: 1-800-HAWORTH. E-mail address: <docdelivery@haworthpress. com> Website: <http://www.HaworthPress.com> © 2003 by The Haworth Press, Inc. All rights reserved.]*

KEYWORDS. Financial development, financial regulation, interest rates

INTRODUCTION

Does it matter that all of the sub-Saharan African countries have small financial systems? In this short paper, we review the reasons why

---

Biagio Bossone is with the Office of the Executive Director, International Monetary Fund, Washington DC, 20431 (E-mail: bbossone@imf.org). Patrick Honohan is with the World Bank, 1818 H Street NW, Washington DC 20433 (E-mail: phonohan@ worldbank.org).

[Haworth co-indexing entry note]: "Coping with a Small Financial System: Policy Issues for Africa." Bossone, Biagio, and Patrick Honohan. Co-published simultaneously in *Journal of African Business* (International Business Press, an imprint of The Haworth Press, Inc.) Vol. 4, No. 2, 2003, pp. 5-20; and: *African Business Finance and Development Policy* (eds: Victor Murinde and Atsede Woldie) International Business Press, an imprint of The Haworth Press, Inc., 2003, pp. 5-20. Single or multiple copies of this article are available for a fee from The Haworth Document Delivery Service [1-800-HAWORTH, 9:00 a.m. - 5:00 p.m. (EST). E-mail address: docdelivery@haworthpress.com].

size is relevant, and consider some of the possible ways of alleviating the problems resulting from having a small financial system. One of the potential solutions is regional cooperation. This has already been tried, with a degree of success, in parts of Africa. More could be done.

The paper begins by drawing on recent analysis of the issues surrounding financial sector policy that are specific to small systems. We ask which financial systems are small, what are the particular problems they face, and what are the potential solutions. To illustrate the quantitative relevance of the points, we take the case of bank interest spreads (in the second section), showing a tendency for them to be wider in small financial systems.

We then proceed to describe (in the third section) some of the efforts made in Africa to overcome these problems through regional cooperation. The fourth section looks at one alternative approach to regional cooperation or outsourcing, relying more on private initiative. The fifth section concludes.

POLICY FOR SMALL FINANCIAL SYSTEMS

The Problem[1]

In finance, being very small in size is seldom efficient. We already know from an extensive literature that small *economies* are volatile and prone to lumpiness, though they are not especially poor or slow-growing (Easterly and Kraay, 2000). The ability of financial systems in such economies to diversify risk and to provide adequate liquidity is limited. Diseconomies of scale prevail both at the production level of individual intermediaries and at the level of financial infrastructural components. For this reason, financial services in these systems tend to be more expensive and of poorer quality, thereby limiting development (Bossone, Honohan and Long, 2000). In addition, small *financial systems* are less competitive (as we will illustrate in the next section), incomplete (in terms of the range of services they provide), and more costly to regulate and supervise. To some extent, openness can offset the drawbacks of small size, but achieving adequate opening without undue risk needs some carefully tailored policy design.

The issue of policy for small financial systems is not a curiosum applying only to a handful of countries of negligible aggregate importance. Many financial systems are extremely small. About 60 countries have financial systems each of whose total size (measured in terms of

M2) is less than $1 billion, no larger than a small bank in an industrial country. Indeed more than half of World Bank/IDA borrowers fall below the somewhat higher threshold of $10 billion, and these countries account for a total population of 800 million persons. Some of the economies that have a large population can be expected, over time and with improvements in overall policy and development, to experience financial deepening (and this, in turn, will contribute to their growth), but countries with small populations cannot be expected to develop large financial sectors–at least those exclusively serving the domestic market.

Most discussions of financial sector policy do not seem to involve any systematic differentiation on grounds of size. Yet it appears that the optimal design of regulatory institutions and practices, as well as competition and entry policies, need to be different as between small and large countries. Conventional financial sector policy thinking is implicitly calibrated on a reasonably large economy within which the fixed overhead costs of regulatory institutions are not a major consideration, in which enough intermediaries and markets can achieve minimum efficient scale within a competitive system, and in which there is a good diversity of financial assets and prospects to allow risk-pooling. Some regulations arguably need to be modified to make them suitable to small financial systems.

Openness as a Solution

Many of the disadvantages of small financial size can be mitigated through various forms of openness, that is, through integration into a larger system. Here several different dimensions of openness are especially relevant, including cross-border trade in financial flows and services, foreign ownership of financial intermediaries, and regional/international cooperation in the establishment of financial infrastructure and in the operation of financial markets and intermediaries.[2] Each of these forms may have advantages, depending upon the problem to be resolved, and they may be supplemented by other actions such as adoption of a common currency, or tailored prudential regulations reflecting special circumstances.

However, openness does pose some disadvantages, too: it may increase the volatility of capital flows, it may reduce the quantity of investable resources, and it almost certainly leads to a loss of autonomy and increases the dangers of contagion. Hence, there needs to be some caution in opening-up finance in these various dimensions.

Furthermore, some dimensions of openness are not available to all countries; for example, small poor countries may find it impossible to attract high quality, foreign financial institutions to open facilities. But most small financial systems have not opened-up enough. The various possibilities need to be explored with sensitivity to national conditions (see Table 1).

Foreign Ownership of Intermediaries

Although small financial systems tend to have a somewhat higher share of foreign ownership, there is indeed much scope for further opening. Despite traditional populist resistance to foreign-controlled finance, the recent wave of foreign acquisition of banks has convinced many countries of the benefits to economic activity, efficiency and stability of having foreign-owned financial intermediaries. The presence of foreign banks can be stabilizing in a crisis, and entry of foreign banks can make national banking markets more competitive, in that the higher the share of foreign-owned banks, the lower the profits and overhead expenses of domestically-owned banks (Claessens, Demirgüç-Kunt and Huizinga, 2001). The context here has been accelerated somewhat by developments in the WTO and GATS (cf. Murinde and Ryan, 2001).

Regional Securities Markets

The arrival of the euro, combined with communications technology developments, have accelerated the process of international consolida-

TABLE 1. Possible Solutions

Possible Solution	Problem
Foreign ownership of intermediaries	Lack of competition; high intermediation costs; inadequate management and governance; inadequate supervision; missing financial products
Regional securities markets	Limited growth potential for (and low franchise of) market intermediaries; poor risk diversification and high vulnerability to shocks; limited interest from foreign investors
Shared regional infrastructure, or imported infrastructural services (including regulation)	Absence or low quality of elements of infrastructure due to high set-up costs; lack of competition; problems of ensuring operational independence of regulators
Tailored regulations	Normal regulatory parameters unsuited to small systems; higher financial fragility
Open capital flows	Lumpy projects; inadequate diversification (risk, insider lending)
Common (or foreign) currency	High risk and cost on cross-border transactions

tion of securities exchanges in Europe through cross-border mergers and joint ventures. This is likely a harbinger of things to come in the rest of the world, with regional stock markets already operating or being put in place in West Africa, the Gulf and the Baltic/Nordic countries. Regional markets could provide the jumpstarting necessary for small intermediaries to achieve the critical scale to become financially viable and to internationalize their activity. With the possibility of foreign listing open to larger companies, the role even of regional exchanges in the Developing World may be focused on medium-size companies.

Shared Regional Infrastructure

Both to reach minimum efficient scale, as well as to help support regional markets, there is much to be gained from moving towards various forms of shared financial infrastructural capacity, including common standardized components (payment and settlement systems provide a good example).

A regional approach also to prudential supervision and regulation could allow the regulators to be better shielded than national authorities from pressure to compromise on prudential standards, or to delay or deny action on problem institutions especially in small systems where regulators and regulatees are at less than arms' length distance from each other. Also, regional organizations might prove more effective in resolving "coordination failure" problems in the event of crises, when no national authority may be prepared to take the lead and act.

Regional infrastructures should enable intermediaries located in each participating country to sell and deliver their products and services anywhere in the region at no cost disadvantage with respect to their competitors in the region. While success in promoting regional cooperation has not always been achieved, experience shows that effective regional cooperation in focused areas can also help lead in time to further and wider forms of cooperation between the governments in the region.

Importing Financial (Infrastructural) Services from Abroad

When "going regional" is not an option, a small financial system may benefit from importing key financial infrastructural services from larger and more developed countries. For example, domestic institutions could be given remote access to more efficient settlement facilities located abroad, and be allowed to subcontract internationally for specialized services. Also, foreign providers could be permitted to supply cross-border services to domestic users from remote, financial contracts may be signed under the jurisdiction of another country, and financial firms may be required to be branches of licensed institutions in well-supervised countries.

So far there does not seem to be much evidence of this happening, perhaps because of a view that conflicts of interest could arise if an international consultancy firm were used to carry out, say, bank inspections. But this may in many cases be a rational way to move forward, not only for banks, but perhaps especially for specialized financial institutions such as insurance or securities markets, where the need for heavy resource use would be especially sporadic. The rapidly developing role and potential of information technology (e-finance) can offer an important way forward for small financial systems, with the potential to reduce greatly their isolation from the world financial system.

Openness May Call for Tailored Regulations

Careful design in particular of prudential rules (such as capital adequacy and liquidity requirements) is required to ensure that the relatively greater fragility of small financial systems is adequately taken into account, and also of competition policy to offset the heightened risk of abuse of market power in small markets.

BANK INTEREST SPREADS
AND THE SIZE OF THE FINANCIAL SYSTEM

It may be worth looking briefly at some quantitative evidence showing that financial system size matters. Consider the question of banking spreads: a look at the data does suggest that smaller financial systems are less competitive. Figure 1 plots the quoted interest rate spreads (lending minus deposit rates) against the dollar value (measured in logs) of broad money for the 108 countries for which this data is available in *International Financial Statistics* for 1998. While the scatter is very wide, reflecting the many influences on spread, as well as the imperfections of the data, a downward slope is evident, suggesting that larger financial systems tend to have lower spreads and as such may be more efficient and competitive. Note that the explanatory variable is not financial *depth* normalized by GDP, but financial *size*.

Regression analysis confirms the visual impression: a negative coefficient is obtained on the scale variable. While this is not statistically

FIGURE 1. Quoted Interest Rate Spread and Size of Financial Sector

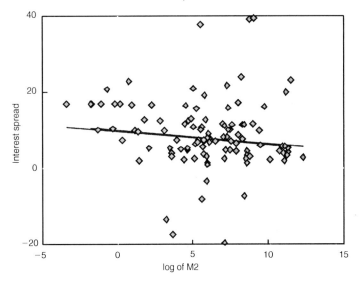

—Regression line (based on regression including gnp per cap)

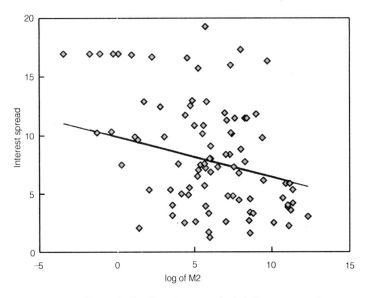

—Regression line (based on regression including gnp per cap)

significant on the whole sample, it is highly significant once we filter out the countries with negative spreads and those with very high spreads (above about 2000 basis points–still leaving between 80 and 90 countries, depending on whether the countries of the BEAC zone are all included separately). Of course, financial size is correlated with level of development (per capita GNP), which in turn could be causally associated with lower spreads. In order to verify that the negative coefficient estimated for financial size does not simply reflect level of development, we included this in the equation also. Furthermore, we included the nominal deposit interest rate and recent inflation as control variables, to take account of the wider spreads that are often associated with higher financial uncertainty. The significance of financial size remains high (t-statistic = 2.4, implying statistical significance at the 2 per cent level), and the economic significance of the effect is sizable. The point estimates implies that a doubling of financial size would lower bank interest spreads by between 21 and 40 basis points.

These findings, though they can only be regarded as suggestive, raise the intriguing possibility that expanding the scale of a country's financial system, perhaps by entering into a financial union, could result in impressive gains in static economic efficiency. After all, the predicted gain from quadrupling the effective size of a small country's banking system when applied to aggregate balance sheets amounting to say 50 per cent of GDP ranges from 2 to 4 per cent of GDP per annum.

THE POSITION IN AFRICA

When we turn to consider the situation in Africa, we recognize that it is in Sub-Saharan Africa that we find the largest concentration of small financial systems. As we can see from Table 2, not a single financial system here (RSA aside) has a value of the monetary aggregate M2 that exceeds $10 billion–the size of quite a modest bank in most industrial countries. (To put this another way, and perhaps slightly unfairly, the total balance sheet of the Skipton Building Society in Yorkshire was far larger at end-1999 than the entire Nigerian banking system.)

So what's to be done? One obvious potential approach, which has already been applied in Africa, is the regional one. The best-known example is the use of a common currency in West Africa, but financial sector cooperation has gone deeper. Let's consider two key examples of what has been done.

TABLE 2. Size of Financial Systems in Sub-Saharan Africa (alphabetical order)

	World rank	M2 $ million	GDP $ million	Population million		World rank	M2 $ million	GDP $ million	Population million
Angola	52	900	7662	11.7	Liberia	47	696	3422	2.9
Benin	41	489	2120	5.8	Madagascar	25	279	1965	14.1
Botswana	56	1077	4729	1.5	Malawi	43	577	2391	10.3
Burkina Faso	44	588	2146	10.9	Mali	12	158		10.3
Burundi	14	167	790	6.6	Mauritania				2.4
Cameroon	59	1155	8379	14.1	Mauritius	82	3092	3917	1.1
Cape Verde	29	315	425	0.4	Mozambique	49	719		18.5
Central African Rep.	18	194	1019	3.4	Namibia	60	1322	3280	1.6
Chad	17	191	1603	6.8	Niger	13	164	1540	9.7
Comoros	4	41	194	0.5	Nigeria	92	7145		109.0
Congo, Rep.	33	337	2298	2.8	Rwanda	26	290	1843	7.9
Cote d'Ivoire	78	2685	10025	14.7	Sao Tome & Principe	1	12	44	0.1
Djibouti	30	317	500	0.6	Senegal	54	968	4427	8.8
Equatorial Guinea	2	30	487	0.4	Seychelles	37	388	528	0.1
Eritrea				3.8	Sierra Leone	8	95	823	4.7
Ethiopia	77	2668	6041	60.1	Sudan	53	917	9299	27.9
Gabon	50	782	5153	1.2	Swaziland	34	350	1242	1.0
Gambia, The	9	113	407	1.2	Tanzania	64	1484		31.3
Ghana	58	1154	6210	18.0	Togo	32	329	1365	4.3
Guinea	35	363	3688	6.9	Uganda	48	705		20.3
Guinea Bissau	3	30	266	0.7	Zambia	46	622	3558	9.4
Kenya	89	4446	9596	28.0	Zimbabwe	67	1670	8906	11.5
Lesotho	27	298	843	2.1					

Building Up Regional Financial Infrastructure in Southern Africa

One of the most interesting examples of national governments cooperating to build-up common regional infrastructure is the South African Development Community (SADC). The SADC aims[3] at harmonizing the components of national financial infrastructural components with a view to pursuing regional economic and political integration. The organization works to select and discuss ideas for common projects, to build-up consensus on operational strategies and targets, to ensure capacity building in each member country, and to follow-up on project implementation. Each of the member countries of the SADC (Angola, Botswana, Democratic Republic of Congo, Lesotho, Malawi, Mozambique, Mauritius, Namibia, Seychelles, South Africa, Swaziland, Tanzania, Zambia, and Zimbabwe) is responsible for coordinating regional cooperation in specific sector(s). South Africa is responsible for the Finance and Investment Sector. Within such sector, the Committee of Central Bank Governors (CCBG) is mandated to focus on closer cooperation in the areas of monetary policy; bank supervision; money and capital markets; payment, clearing, and settlement systems; and money laundering.

Since its inception in 1995, the CCBG has initiated a number of projects ranging from the development of a monetary and financial statistical database to the establishment of a standardized legal and operational framework for central banks, to the development of common information technology, the creation of a common platform for protective services, and the enhancement of domestic money markets. Each project ensures that the existing domestic infrastructural components are gradually harmonized, and that new infrastructural components are mutually compatible so as to allow for future integration. The CCBG is currently coordinating payment system project with the assistance of the World Bank. The main objectives of the project are, firstly, to assist the individual SADC countries to define a domestic payment strategy and a development plan for the reform of their payment systems and, secondly, to define a regional approach to cross-border payments.

Important steps are being taken by the SADC also in the area of stock exchanges and bond markets. Member countries are harmonizing access and listing requirements to make the region more accessible to external investors and the procedures for trading, clearing, and settling stock exchange transactions. Also, they have agreed to allow for regional sharing of local infrastructure (such as bond exchanges and depository facilities in certain countries) when re-organizing domestic bond markets, while they are considering to set up centralized capital markets.

Cooperative Financial Sector Arrangements in the CFA Franc Zone

Although sometimes seen as part of the post-Colonial inheritance, and though the member countries were, by the late 1980s, mired in recession, illiquidity and widespread bank insolvency, the two African unions of the franc zone[4] received a new lease of life from the early 1990s. A wave of institutional renewal, partly inspired by the near contemporary deepening of the multi-national institutions of the European Union, was weighted towards financial cooperation.

New treaties and agreements both reformed existing structures, including the two regional central banks BCEAO and BEAC[5], and established a host of new entities, several of which extended across the whole of the franc zone, without distinction between West and Central. These include: the Inter-African Conference on Insurance Markets (CIMA)[6], the Inter-African Conference on Social Security (CIPRES), the two regional banking commissions, the regional stock exchange, the Organization for the Harmonization of Business Law in Africa (OHADA)[7], the West African Accounting System (SYSCOA) and AFRISTAT.

A feature of the new institutions is the degree to which the headquarters have been distributed among the various member states. Thus, for example, while the headquarters of the BEAC has long been Yaounde (Cameroon), that of the COBAC is in Libreville (Gabon), and the headquarters of the monetary union itself UMAC is in Bangui (CAR). Likewise the BCEAO is based in Dakar (Senegal) while the Banking Commission of the UEMOA is based in Abidjan (Cote d'Ivoire).

Among the most interesting of the new institutions for the present context are the regional banking commissions (both established by agreements signed in 1990), the regional stock exchange, and the proposed regional payment system.

By centralizing the function of *bank regulation and supervision*, the member states sought to centralize scarce supervisory resources and also to distance the function from national pressures (hitherto, the function had been a national concern). The two banking commissions are independent, though each differs in its constitution and in its powers. The Banking Commission for Central Africa (COBAC) started functioning in January 1993. The Commission has eleven members, of which seven come from the member states and three from the BEAC itself (all of these are nominated by the Governor of BEAC, who also chairs the Commission). The eleventh seat is taken by a nominee of the Governor of the Banque de France. With their small staff (of 22 in 1996), the COBAC sets regulations and carries out on- and off-site supervision of the region's 32 banks, 17 finance houses (and 22 further banks in liquidation). It has a wide and graduated range of sanctions available to it, including warnings, reprimands, cease and desist orders, dismissal of auditors or managers and, significantly, withdrawal of license. The professionalism of the COBAC is widely admired, though bank soundness remains problematic in the zone. For example, Cameroon saw a wave of bank recapitalization in 1995-96, the second within a decade, and in 1999 a half of Cameroon's banks were still said to be either fragile or in a critical situation.

The Banking Commission of the UEMOA is also chaired by the Governor of the regional central bank and comprises eight nominees of the member governments and eight of the BCEAO. There is no nominee of the Banque de France. Its rather larger staff (80 in 1996) regulates and supervises 61 banks and 29 finance houses.

It might have been thought that a common regime of bank supervision and regulation might have helped boost confidence in banking across borders within the two unions, but in practice interbank markets are very inactive. Interbank transactions across borders are essentially confined to affiliates of the same banking group, and even the negotiable certificates of deposit issues by the BEAC have not been much used as security for interbank transactions, apparently reflecting their uncertain legal status.

Establishment of the *Regional Stock Exchange* (BRVM) was agreed by the UEMOA member states in 1992, and preparations continued to develop this from the basis of the Abidjan stock exchange, which had been functioning since 1976. The regional exchange opened in September 1998. Regulation and supervision is by an organ of the UEMOA called the Regional Council of Public Savings and of Markets (CREPM). Operation of the exchange has been granted to a private company owned by Stock Exchange Companies (Management and Investment Companies–of which 14 have been licensed)[8] (63%), other financial institutions (23%) and the member states (14%). While the exchange is in Abidjan, there is a network allowing orders from all of the member states to be centralized. There are three sessions per week, and two electronic fixings per session; settlement is T + 5 and all shares are dematerialized. A central depository and settlement bank is owned by the same shareholders who own the BRVM itself.

By mid-1999, progress towards expanding the market into a truly regional one had been limited. Two new shares had been added to the 35 already on the Abidjan exchange[9], of which one (the only non-Ivorian share) was sonatel, the Senegal telephone company, which alone accounted for one quarter of a total market capitalization of FCFA 1165 billion ($2 billion). This total capitalization is less than 7 per cent of the UEMOA GDP. Annualized turnover for the first half of 1999 was only 5 per cent, very low by international standards. The primary bond market was somewhat more active, with seven new issues during the first nine months of the exchange's operation for a total of FCFA 50 billion (about $100 million); the issuers were the West African regional development bank BOAD, the Ivorian treasury and the Cote d'Ivoire and Senegal affiliates of SGB bank. The secondary bond market was, however, practically inactive with a daily average trade of scarcely FCFA 100,000 (about $200), and a maximum daily trade of FCFA 25 million ($50,000).

The UEMOA is also planning to set-up a regionally integrated *payment system* (with the assistance of the World Bank). The new system, which will replace the current slow, unreliable, and costly payment systems, will incorporate a number of components for the efficient and safe execution of large- and small-value payments and for the launch of a pilot scheme for using e-money (smart cards) for small payments typically made by poor people. The system will also incorporate a legal framework including inter-bank rules and procedures to ensure fully compatible transaction processing from one participant to another across the region. The new system is expected to provide essential support for the development of regional inter-bank deposit and capital markets.

ALTERNATIVE APPROACHES FOR INTEGRATION

These examples both illustrate what can be done and some of the limitations. It is worth bearing in mind some alternative institutional approaches that could be adopted to develop regional cooperation on banking regulation and supervision. The above-mentioned approaches are based on government-led initiatives. Indeed, where the political will exists among national governments in a region to move toward full-fledged cooperation, a regional public authority can be established where each national government is represented and which is entrusted with the responsibility to determine prudential rules and regulations, and to supervise their adoption by individual banks throughout the region. A potential drawback of this type of arrangement is that it requires an abdication of national sovereignty: sanctioning a bank may have such serious adverse implications for the economy in which it primarily operates that the national authority wants to retain the freedom to weigh the consequences of the sanction against the consequences of taking lighter action. As a result, a jump to a regional, public sector solution might be (politically) difficult to achieve.

In the absence of government action, the market itself can play a role by establishing a regional private-sector authority, with public functions (see Folkerts-Landau and van Greuning, 1997). Reputable and sound banks can volunteer to submit their operations to scrutiny by a private entity, much as they do for external audits, for clearing payment and securities transactions, and for acquiring and maintaining a credit rating. Individual banks could agree to abide to a common code of conduct including standards based on transparent prudential criteria. A private regional authority would be molded from within the banking industry itself and act as a self-regulatory body (Bossone and Promisel, 1999) that would receive evidence from members of their adherence to the code of conduct and publish the results. So long as the major players accept to adhere to the code, others would be induced to conform. The mechanism could generate stronger incentives for individual banks to improve their responsiveness to prudential requirements than unilateral national rules, which might place banks at a competitive disadvantage. The very existence of regional private sector initiatives with public purpose might solicit (if not force) national governments to elaborate regional cooperative strategies.

CONCLUDING REMARKS

Small financial systems are more likely to have incomplete financial markets. In small financial systems, intermediaries may operate at suboptimal scales and may lack access to efficient infrastructure. Borrowers are likely to lack access to existing services, and those services that are available are likely to be of poorer quality and more expensive. Risk is less well diversified, and the supervisory institutions are less able to do their job. All of this raises the issue of the extent to which these problems can be overcome through some form of openness.

We have argued that there is a lot to be gained from carefully encouraging increased openness to foreign ownership of financial intermediaries, and from exploring regional solutions in terms both of markets and financial infrastructure. Importing elements of financial infrastructure from (more efficient) foreign providers could be a valuable option. Greater openness may call for tailored regulation in terms of prudential rules, competition policy and establishing frameworks that improve liquidity, possibly including innovative financial engineering. Macro solutions such as opening the capital account and choice of exchange rate regime are also very relevant.[10]

NOTES

1. This part of the paper draws on the authors' joint work with Millard Long.
2. As used here, this term includes such elements as: legal and regulatory frameworks (including contract enforcement mechanisms); central banking services; supervision, accounting and auditing rules, resources, and practices; information provision (e.g., credit bureaus, rating agencies, public registries, market analysts); payment and securities settlement systems; exchange systems (e.g., trading and listing services, trading rules, communication/information platforms).
3. This section draws on the Committee of Central Bank Governors of the SADC (*www.sadcbankers.org*).
4. The UEMOA in West Africa comprises Benin, Burkina Faso, Côte d'Ivoire, Mali, Niger, Senegal, Togo and, since 1997, Guinea-Bissau. The CEMAC in Central Africa comprises Cameroon, Central African Republic, Chad, Congo, Equatorial Guinea and Gabon. The Comoros is also a member of the Franc zone.
5. Among the reforms of the BEAC are the enhanced role of the Governor, who now chairs the Conseil d'Administration (instead of a government minister), and the fact that lending to governments now subject to the BEAC's normal refinance rate.
6. This aims to reinforce cooperation and to harmonize law and regulation among member states. A regional commission for insurance regulation started operations in 1996.
7. In addition to the 15 franc zone countries, Guinea (Conakry) is a member of this organization, which is open to any African country.
8. Seven in Cote d'Ivoire, three in Benin and one each in Burkina Faso, Mali, Senegal and Togo.
9. There are two lists, one requiring a minimum capital of FCFA 500 million and a net profit in excess of 3% (23 companies); the other requiring a minimum capital of FCFA 200 million.
10. The question of common currencies in Africa, especially in light of the euro, is discussed in Honohan and Lane (2001).

REFERENCES

Bossone, B., Honohan, P. and Long, M. (2000). "Policy for Small Financial Systems," *World Bank Financial Sector Discussion Paper* 6.
Bossone, B., and L. Promisel (1999). "Self regulation in developing countries," World Bank Financial Sector Website Policy Note (Washington DC: The World Bank). wbwebapps2.worldbank.org/wwwfinance/html/self-regulation-in-developing-.html

Claessens, S., A. Demirgüç-Kunt and H. Huizinga (1998). "How does foreign entry affect the domestic banking market?" World Bank Policy Research Working Paper 1918 (Washington DC: The World Bank).

Easterly, W. and Kraay (2000). "Small states, small problems?" *World Development,* 28 (11): 2013-2027.

Folkerts-Landau, E. and Van Greuning, H. (1997). "The case for regional financial-market infrastructure in Africa. How Africa's financial systems could move toward greater regional integration," Washington DC: The World Bank, April. (mimeo).

Honohan, P. and Lane, P. (2001). "Will the euro trigger more monetary unions in Africa?" in *EMU: Impact on Europe and the Developing Countries*: Wyplosz, C. (ed.), Oxford University Press, pp. 315-338.

Murinde, V. and Ryan, C. (2001). "The implications of WTO and GATS for the banking sector in Africa," in *The Free Trade Area of the Common Market for Eastern and Southern Africa*: Murinde, V. (ed.), Aldershot: Ashgate, pp. 135-169.

The Design, Development and Implementation of Bank Licensing Policies and Procedures in Zambia (1980-2000)

Samuel Munzele Maimbo

SUMMARY. This study reviews the design, development and implementation of licensing policies in the years preceding the 1995-1997/98 bank failures in Zambia (1980-1994), and the licensing reforms that were followed thereafter (1995-2000). It documents important weaknesses in licensing practices that hindered regulatory effectiveness: inadequate minimum capital standards, insufficient ownership/management quality assessments, inadequate consideration of the convenience and needs of the financial sector and political interference in the licensing process. In addressing these and other weaknesses, however, the paper calls for research on prudential entry requirements to go beyond identifying desirable minimum requirements to establishing practical tools

Samuel Munzele Maimbo is Financial Analyst, World Bank, Banking and Financial Restructuring Department, Room MC9-770 (Mail stop MC9-907), The World Bank, 1818H Street NW, Washington, DC 20433 (E-mail: smaimbo@worldbank.org).

The findings, interpretations, and conclusions expressed in this paper are entirely those of the author and do not necessarily represent the views and policies of the World Bank or its Board of Executive Directors or the countries they represent.

[Haworth co-indexing entry note]: "The Design, Development and Implementation of Bank Licensing Policies and Procedures in Zambia (1980-2000)." Maimbo, Samuel Munzele. Co-published simultaneously in *Journal of African Business* (International Business Press, an imprint of The Haworth Press, Inc.) Vol. 4, No. 2, 2003, pp. 21-45; and: *African Business Finance and Development Policy* (eds: Victor Murinde and Atsede Woldie) International Business Press, an imprint of The Haworth Press, Inc., 2003, pp. 21-45. Single or multiple copies of this article are available for a fee from The Haworth Document Delivery Service [1-800-HAWORTH, 9:00 a.m. - 5:00 p.m. (EST). E-mail address: docdelivery@haworthpress.com].

and techniques for regulators, especially for evaluating the quality of prospective bank owners and managers. It nevertheless cautions against adopting an overly cautious licensing policy, especially towards domestic banks as they provide valuable services to domestic economies. *[Article copies available for a fee from The Haworth Document Delivery Service: 1-800-HAWORTH. E-mail address: <docdelivery@haworthpress.com> Website: <http://www.HaworthPress.com> © 2003 by The Haworth Press, Inc. All rights reserved.]*

KEYWORDS. Licensing policies, bank ownership, minimum capital, management quality

INTRODUCTION

Bank licensing policies and procedures are an important aspect of the development of the financial sector. The design, development and implementation of effective entry regulations contribute significantly to the structure and quality of the banking sector. Although there exists an extensive literature on liberalising entry into the financial sector for purposes of fostering financial sector development, and in turn, economic development, there is a very limited academic literature that discusses the implementation of licensing policies and procedures. Moreover, that literature often does not proceed beyond addressing the desirable characteristics of potential banks and their owners. Although a subsidiary body of literature has emerged that considers the impact of foreign banks entering the domestic banking system of a developing economy (Classens et al., 1998; Brownbridge and Gockel, 1996; Harvey, 1996), that literature does not systematically consider the steps regulators take in processing their license applications.

Along these lines, the paper examines the design, development and implementation of the bank licensing process in the immediate years before the 1995-1997/98 bank failures. It argues that the weaknesses in the licensing policies and procedures were significant contributing factors to those failures because of insufficient regard given to the quality of prospective owners, directors and managers, the amount of capital required, and the development of reasonable business plans. Its thesis is that regulatory failure occurred at the licensing stage in the light of the failure of the Registrar of Banks (the Registrar) to minimise the risk of unsuitably qualified individuals gaining access to banking licenses.

Section 2 outlines the paper's research methods. Section 3 highlights the recent literature on what is generally accepted best practice for licensing banks. Then Section 4 focuses on the MoF licensing handling of twenty bank license applications (1980-1994). Thereafter, Section 5 discusses the 1994 bank licensing reforms introduced by the Banking and Financial Services Act, 1994 (BFSA, 1994). It also traces the subsequent changes to the licensing process that the BoZ introduced after the 1995-1997/98 bank failures. Finally, Section 6 considers the efficacy of the recent bank licensing reforms before presenting the paper's conclusions.

RESEARCH METHODOLOGY

This paper is the product of a four month field trip to Zambia (May-August 2000) which composed of three principal activities, namely, documentary review, interviews and a workshop with BoZ staff. The first activity involved a detailed documentary investigation of 20 licence applications submitted to the Ministry of Finance (MoF) and the BoZ (1990-1994). Six licences of banks that have not failed and fourteen licences, which BoZ approved but subsequently revoked. Other documents examined included relevant banking laws, regulatory policy statements, World Bank and BoZ supervisory reports, legal case documents, and where possible, correspondence between the BoZ and license applications. The second phase involved in-depth interviews with a selection of key respondents which included former BoZ Governors, Former Directors of the Financial System Supervision Department (FSSD), Assistant Directors, bank inspectors, former owners and directors of failed banks, civil servants, bank management, officials from other regulatory bodies and other key contact persons were included in the choice of interview respondents. The sample of twenty- eight interviews embraced a sufficient heterogeneity of experiences and accounts within the constraints of money and time. Lastly, the study organised a one-day workshop for fifteen senior BoZ inspectors. The workshop provided a forum at which the researcher discussed the findings of the visit with the inspectors. The recorded transcripts of the workshop discussions form an important part of the qualitative data collection process.

An issue of major concern throughout the research visit was the desire to maintain and respect the confidential nature of the information, which the BoZ made available for the study. For that reason individual banks and officers involved in the licensing process are not named.

ENTRY REGULATIONS IN BANKING

The prudential regulatory process commences with the screening of license applicants in order to prevent those with inappropriate professional qualifications, banking experience, financial capacity and ethical backgrounds from owning/managing banks. Polizatto (1990: 176) recommended that, at a minimum, prudential entry regulations should address the issues of capital, management qualifications, and the development of a reasonable business plan. To reduce political interference, he further recommended that independent supervisory authorities are responsible for bank licensing. David Folkerts-Landau and Carl Johan Lindgren (1997:17) noted that the licensing process set out in the banking laws of IMF member countries verified five principle issues, namely, the sufficiency of a bank's initial capital, the suitability of major shareholders and management and the transparency of its corporate and organisation structure. In the case of foreign banks, that the bank received adequate supervision in its home country and the home country regulator approved the establishment of the branch.

The Core Principles for Effective Banking Supervision, issued in September 1997, by the Basel Committee on Banking Supervision (BCBS) recognise the importance of the licensing process in Principle 3, which states that: "The licensing authority must have the right to set criteria and reject applications for establishments that do not meet the standards set. The licensing process should consist of an assessment of the bank's ownership structure, directors and senior management, its operating plan and internal controls, and its projected financial condition, including its capital base. Where the proposed owner or parent organisation is a foreign bank, the prior consent of its home country should be obtained."

Minimum Capital Requirements

The literature on minimum bank capital focuses on two principle issues. Firstly, how to define capital. Secondly, how to measure its adequacy (Revell, 1979; Howard, 1980; Gardener, 1979; Berger, 1995; BCBS, 1988; Llewellyn, 1992; Benston, 1992; Blum, 1995; Shah, 1996; Jackson et al., 1999; BCBS, 1999). The most significant contribution to the literature on capital adequacy, however, was the 1988 BCBS Capital Accord circulated initially to BCBS member countries and subsequently adopted by the majority of countries around the world. In attempting to establish a standard definition of capital with specific proposals on its measurement, the committee consolidated the research issues on capital adequacy into a single document that henceforth became a reference point. Thereafter, the increasing body of literature focused on criticising the 1988 Capital Accord (Benston, 1992; Calomiris, 1992, 1998; Shah, 1996; Jackson and Perraundin, 1998; BCBS, 1999), which finally resulted in amendments to the 1998 Accord and proposals for a New Capital Adequacy Framework in June 1999 (BCBS, 2001).

The issues that arise out of the new capital adequacy framework are exactly the same issues that have been raised in the literature over the last few decades. How should bank capital be defined? What level of capital is adequate for banks to remain safe and sound? What criteria should be used to assess the adequacy of capital? Short (1978) aptly observed that "The length of time that capital adequacy has been debated suggests the extreme difficulty, really the impossibility, of objectively deciding what is an adequate amount of capital, or what is the appropriate ratio of capital to assets, liabilities, deposits, or risk assets—whichever denominator is eventually chosen." Although the committee prepared the regulations for large international banks operating in OECD countries, most developing countries have adopted the Basle capital recommendations as a local standard for domestic and foreign banks operating within their jurisdiction. The minimum capital required to open a bank is thus the higher of 8% of total risk weighted capital or an absolute amount, whose determination varies across different countries.

Character, Financial Condition, History, and Experience of Applicants

The assessment and regulation of the quality of bank shareholders is perhaps the most challenging aspect of a regulators work. Despite the best risk management tools and techniques, banks will fail under the weight of weak owners/managers. Being a subjective matter, it is difficult to assess and even harder to set objective criteria for its assessment (Goodhart, 1995: 25). How can regulators impose regulatory standards on human quality and managerial skill and culture?

Mehran et al. (1998), in a study of 32 selected sub-Saharan African countries, found that despite a large number of countries enacting new, and quite often detailed, bank licensing legislation, the right of the supervisor to conduct fitness and probity tests was less than fully covered. One of the primary reasons for this deficiency is that licensing standards vary considerably.

The Bank of England's Schedule 3 of the Banking Act 1987 (Box 1) is a typical example of legislation incorporated for this purpose. The difficulty with Schedule 3, and similar legislation like it, is that some sections are difficult to verify and thus left to the discretionary interpretation of regulators. For example, Parts 3(a) and 3(b) of Schedule 3 are easily verifiable by a search done at the courts. However, that is not the case with parts 3(c) and 3(d), which are subject to different interpretations. It is not surprising, therefore, that in some countries, applicants will seek political influence or offer financial incentives to regulators in order to ensure that such discretionary pieces of legislation are "interpreted correctly."

Another concern in the literature on bank ownership relates to the desirability and extent of foreign ownership of banks, especially the effect foreign banks have on domestic banks. Regulators have adopted varying approaches to this issue. In some countries, there is a lower minimum start up capital requirement for local banks in order to encourage local participation in banking business. In other countries, however, the banking sector is closed to foreign banks (Brownbridge and Gockel, 1996; Harvey, 1996).

Classens et al. (1998), who examined the effect of foreign banks on domestic banks in 80 countries, concluded that although relaxing the restrictions on foreign bank entry reduced the profits of domestic bank, it had an overall positive welfare effect on the economy. They also observed that it was more the number of banks entering the market rather than their market share that was important. This seemed to suggest, in their opinion, that foreign banks affected local bank competition at the point of entry rather than after they had gained a substantial market share.

Convenience and Needs of the Community

The licensing criteria regulators use has implications on the franchise value applicants attach to the licence. If the value is substantial, they will take actions to ensure that they keep that licence, the bank remains open, and they continue earning profits with that licence. If the value is

BOX 1. Minimum Criteria for Authorisation of Bank Directors

Banking Act 1987

SCHEDULE 3

MINIMUM CRITERIA FOR AUTHORISATION

Directors, etc., to be fit and proper persons

1.–(1) Every person who is, or is to be, a director, a controller or manager of the institutions is a fit and proper person to hold the particular position which he holds or is to hold.

(2) In determining whether a person is a fit and proper person to hold any particular position, regard shall be had to his probity, his competence and soundness of judgement for fulfilling the responsibilities of that position, to the diligence with which he is fulfilling or likely to fulfil those responsibilities and to whether the interests of depositors or potential depositors of the institutions are or are likely to be, in any way threatened by his holding that position.

(3) Without prejudice to the generality of the foregoing provisions, regard may be had to the previous conduct and activities in business or financial matters of the person in question and, in particular, to any evidence that he has–

    (a)   committed an offence involving fraud or other dishonesty or violence;

    (b)   contravened any provision made by or under any enactment appearing to the Bank to be designed for protecting members of the public against financial loss due to dishonesty, incompetence or malpractice by persons concerned in the provision of banking, insurance, investment or other financial services or the management of companies or against financial loss due to the conduct of discharged or undischarged bankrupts.

    (c)   engaged in any business practices appearing to the Bank to be deceitful or oppressive or otherwise improper (whether unlawful or not) or which otherwise reflect discredit on his method of conducting business;

    (d)   engaged in or been associates with any other business practices in such a way as to cast doubt on his competence and soundness of judgement.

Source: Banking Act 1987

low, then bank owners may engage in riskier business practices. There appears to be an inverse relationship between the franchise value of a license and the bank convenience and needs of the community services. If a community is in need of more banking services, regulators may lower the minimum licensing requirements, which in turn lowers the franchise value of banking licenses.

It has been argued in the literature that banking in the United States became riskier in the 1950s when profits were eroded as a result of the gradual increase in competition from non-banks and foreign banks. The decision to relax the entry requirements into the banking market led to declining profits, the discounted value of which represents the franchise value of possessing a licence. A reduction in the franchise value led to unsafe banking practices as banks engaged in riskier activities to sustain previous profit levels (Caprio, 1996: 15).

One way regulators can preserve the franchise value of licenses is by limiting the number of licenses they grant. In a study of selected Anglophone countries, Harvey (1999) found that some regulatory authorities deliberately limited the number of banking licenses granted in order to protect the existing banks in the financial system. He makes reference to Zimbabwe where the licensing policy was deliberately conservative. The central bank was reluctant to allow new banks into the banking system because it was aware of the problems of newly established banks elsewhere in Africa. The licensing process was deliberately long and involved the Registrar at the MoF, and a committee with representatives from the Inspector of Banks and the Economics Department of the Reserve Bank. The process had many opportunities for the rejection of the application. It appears, however, that the concerns of the regulatory authorities were with the convenience and needs of the existing banks, rather than for the community, which may have benefited from a more competitive environment.

It is difficult to define the number of licences to grant within a given period, and some arbitrariness as to who received the licenses is unavoidable when regulators try to make such a decision. Inevitably, such an approach might lead to an increase in corruption, as bribing regulators can be expected where licences are both valuable and difficult to obtain. In addition, such a restrictive approach may lead to monopolistic rents being accumulated by banks already granted banking licenses (Caprio, 1996: 15-16). From a regulatory perspective, it must be argued that the only purpose of any licensing requirement should be to ensure adequate capitalisation and the availability of sound management, not to limit entry and reduce competition.

Prospects for Profitable Operation of That Business

Standard practice dictates that applications are accompanied by business plans which typically include the applicants planned banking policies, projected earnings, cash flows and expected rates of return. There are, however, a few exceptions to this practice. Harvey (1996: 26) noted a different approach adopted by some regulators in evaluating business plans. The Bank of Botswana, for example, does not attempt to examine the commercial viability of the proposed banks in the belief that the market judgement must be made by the investors whose capital is at risk and not by the licensing authorities. The evaluation of a bank applicant's business plan raises interesting questions for prudential regulatory policy. Is it possible to prescribe detailed regulations on what is an acceptable business plan? Who is better placed to analyse projected bank performance–the central bank, or market participants?

Regulatory Issues in the Licensing Process

Political interference in the evaluation of licence applications hinders the regulators' ability to exercise independent judgement in evaluating applications. Polizatto (1990: 176) noted that in many developing countries licences were granted by government agencies and not those directly responsible for supervising banks.

Mehran et al. (1998) found that in some countries, the central bank shared responsibility for licensing with the MoF or took licensing decisions in consultation with, or with the approval of the Minister of Finance. The arrangement made accountability difficult, increased the risk of subjective judgements and encouraged "rent seeking behaviour" in the process.

In a study of selected Anglophone African countries, Brownbridge (1996: 15) noted that political considerations influenced the granting and renewal of banking licences even when the applicants had not fulfilled the necessary minimum requirements. Instead, the Minister of Finance granted exemptions from some provisions of the Bank Act.

THE EVALUATION OF LICENCE APPLICATIONS IN ZAMBIA (1980-1994)

Introduction

This section discusses the study's findings on the design, development and implementation of bank licensing policies and procedures between 1984 and 1994. The majority of applications examined were for the period 1992-1995 when there was a huge increase in banking liabilities (Figure 1). This section is particularly important because of the substantial rise in the number of banks during that period and also because all the banks that failed in 1995-1997/98 obtained banking licences during this period (Appendix 1).

Minimum Capital Requirements

The study identified five banking practices which indicate that between 1984 and 1994, there was insufficient regard given to the level

FIGURE 1. Growth in Total Deposit Liabilities (1992-1994)

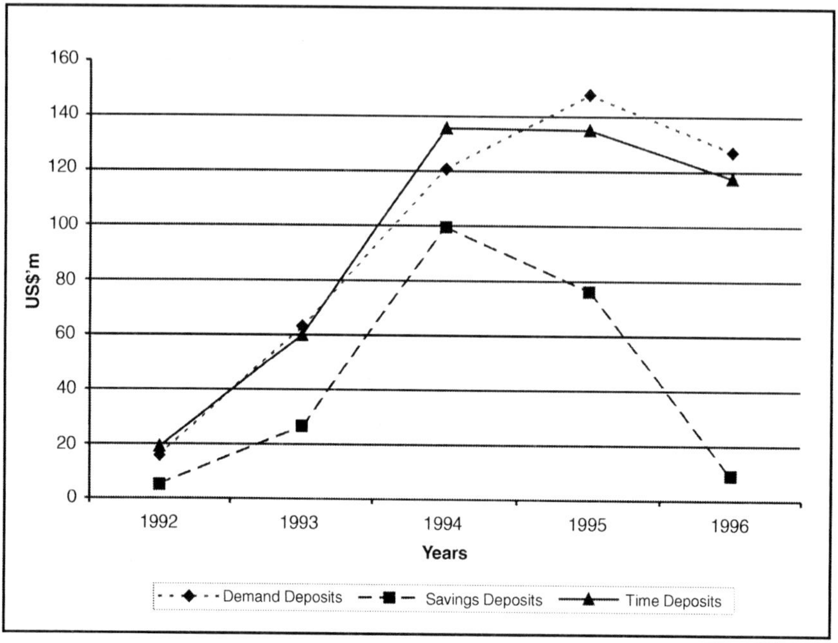

Source: BoZ

and quality of capital of the new banks being licensed. First, throughout that period, the MoF, and later the BoZ, focused on the applicants satisfaction of the legal minimum capital requirement and did not consider the economic and business capital required for a bank to achieve its stated business objectives (Table 1). This is particularly important because, although the minimum capital requirement increased to K20 million from K2 million, inflation had reduced the real value of the minimum requirements to around US$300,000 in 1991 (Brownbridge, 1996: 9).

Second, when required to do so, the majority of banks merely evidenced the availability of the required minimum capital by way of a letter from an existing bank confirming that it held an account on behalf of the promoters to the sum of the required capital at the time. In all these instances the Registrar did not obtain independent third party confirmation of the bank balance.

Third, with the exception of one bank, none of the applicants, who used this form of confirmation, obtained a letter of confirmation from

TABLE 1. Minimum Capital Requirements as of 31 December

Year	K'm	US$'m
1985	2	0.6
1988	2	0.2
1991	20	0.3
1994	1250	1.9
1995	2000	1.8
1996	2000	1.6
1997	2000	1.4
1998	2000	0.8
1999	2000	0.6
2000	2000	0.5

Source: BoZ

one of the larger and more established banks. In fact, five of the nine banks that provided issued letters of confirmation later failed themselves.

Fourth, SITET once arrested one of the directors who had obtained and used one such letter on charges of "false representation" on the amount of capital he had to open his bank. Despite the same bank submitted three different letters from three different banks during the licensing process the MoF favourably considered the application.

Lastly, in at least five cases, the applicants evidenced the existence and availability of capital with only a statement of authorised or paid-up capital signed by their directors. The Registrar did not request any third party confirmation from the bank's auditors. In one case, one bank used a photocopy of a debenture receipt issued by a leasing company owned by the licence applicants. In another, the Registrar granted a licence to a bank on the promise that its shareholders would remit funds to Zambia once the owners received the licence. Although records indicate that the BoZ had "evidence to the effect that funds to the amount of K2m were held in the pipeline awaiting remittance abroad," there is no subsequent evidence to confirm that the funds were ever actually remitted.

Individually, none of the above matters necessarily confirm weaknesses in the licensing process. However, viewed collectively, they suggest sufficient reason to question the sufficiency of the method as an adequate criterion for confirming the level, sufficiency and quality of capital for each bank application.

Financial Condition, Resources and History of Applicants

Before 1992, the MoF did not investigate the applicant's source of the proposed capital. Because the MoF placed greater emphasis on the minimum capital requirement, there was insufficient, import placed on determining the source of funds. In part, that is because, before 1992, a top-down approach to licensing banks prevailed. Politicians often made the decision to approve the application before the documentation reached the Registrar's office and what followed thereafter was a mere formality. The Registrar's responsibility was reduced to ensuring that the applicants submitted the minimum legal documentation and did not include investigating the credibility or authenticity of those documents.

As the number of licence applications increased, however, there was a slight change in that approach. At the request of the then-Minister of Finance, the Registrar started asking applicants to indicate their source of the finances. Although the MoF made this decision in 1993 and the BoZ included it in its 1993 Inspection Handbook which required Bank inspectors to assess "the nature and sufficiency of the financial resources of the applicant or applicants as a source of continuing financial support for the institution," there was no uniformity in the policy's implementation. At best the enquiries were often superficial and did not go further than recording the verbal or written explanations provided by the applicants; there was no independent third party verification of the information the Registrar received.

On the two occasions that the MoF requested for information on the tax status of the group of companies owned by two different entrepreneurial applicants, he was informed that all the companies in the applicants' holding company group had only been registered within that tax year and were yet to pay any taxes. A few applicants chose to submit financial statements of their group companies. However, no reference in either case was made to the cash flow statements and bank statements to assess the financial liquidity of any of the group companies or the availability of on-going financial support. Neither did the applicants submit their bank statements to assess the personal, collective and on-going liquidity.

Character and Experience of Major Shareholders and Directors

Until August 1989, the MoF did not have set criteria for assessing the character and experience of major shareholders and directors. Before then, none of the major shareholders and directors was evaluated for their fitness and probity. In 1989 the MoF determined that the only fair and effective method of assessing the credibility of licence applicants was to subject them to vetting by the country's security institutions–

Ministry of Home Affairs, Anti-Corruption Commission (ACC), Special Investigation Team for Economy and Trade (SITET), and later the Drug Enforcement Commission (DEC). Worse still, the Registrar's requests for applicant's security clearance from the state security departments sometimes went unanswered. In the majority of responses, the state agencies did not have any adverse information about the applicants. In a few cases, the Registrar's requests resulted in adverse information about the applicant's suitability for a banking licence. However, in all three cases, the security departments subsequently cleared the applicants and the Minister of Finance approved their application. Largely, this was due to the lack of evidence upon which the security departments could obtain a conviction in court. The Registrar could only act on actual prior convictions. Mere suspicions, criminal investigation, or insufficient evidence were inadequate to declare an individual unfit to own or manage a bank.

Notwithstanding, the legal argument that an individual was "innocent until proven guilty," the seriousness of the issues for which the security departments were investigating required a measured approach to the approval of their licence application. At a minimum drug trafficking and money laundering, false representation, and fraud should have affected the respective applicant's claim to fitness and probity. More importantly, however, although this vetting process reduced the possibility of known criminals obtaining banking licenses, it gave the misleading impression that anyone who cleared the state security agencies was qualified to own/manage. It also precluded any further analysis of owners' and directors' fitness and probity.

Another matter of concern is the high number of senior BCCI officials that entered the banking system between 1991 and 1994. The MoF made no effort to check if the former BCCI individuals applying for licences had played a role in the closure of the former international bank. One respondent alleged that the BoZ was warned of at least one individual who was previously involved in money laundering. Although the government arrested the individual and had him deported, he later returned to Zambia and carried on in business for a long time. One of the biggest problems for the Registrar was that the applicants were well connected and had a lot of political influence.

The study also noted that the Registrar never returned a bank application to its promoters because of concerns about the integrity of the shareholders or directors; not even when the shareholders and/or directors were involved in, or accused of, grievous criminal activities *during* the licensing process. Instead, the Registrar merely requested the applicants replace the individual concerned and the licensing processing continued. There was no limit to the duration of the process or the number of times the shareholding structure or list of directors changed. In one instance, the Chairman was forced to resign after being arrested on charges of murder. His successor also resigned because the majority shareholder fled the country on hearing that the government was about to deport him for undisclosed reasons. The ownership and management structure changed on each occasion. Despite these events, the Registrar continued to allow changes to the list of shareholders and directors until the application was approved.

Convenience and Needs of the Community

None of the banks included in this study underwent formal assessment to determine their individual contribution to the convenience and needs of the community. Although the MoF repeatedly expressed overall concern about the number of banks entering the financial system, the emphasis was on the applicant's satisfaction of the minimum legal requirements and not whether the bank would make a unique contribution to the banking sector.

There are two reasons for this approach. Firstly, there were no regulatory criteria for assessing a bank's contribution to the community. Secondly, there were no standards for assessing the level of market saturation of the banking system. The first indigenous banks were licensed on a wave of nationalist pride in local entrepreneurial initiatives when they entered a sector hitherto dominated by foreign banks. Whilst the MoF succumbed to these nationalistic, rather than economic sentiments, it resolved to adopt a more cautious approach to any subsequent applications into the banking sector.

In 1986, when another bank was registered, individuals with the MoF again expressed concern about the number of banks in the financial system. Still, in the absence of documented government policy on the required/acceptable number of banks and a standardised formula for measuring the level of market saturation of the banking sector, the Minister of Finance instructed his ministry not to be seen to be standing in the way of any bank promoter who fulfilled the legal requirements. However, dissenting views continued to prevail until the MoF decided to commission a study to formally assess the level of market saturation. Following the 1989 BoZ study which concluded that the banking sector was still open to further competition, the MoF adopted a more open door policy towards licensing banks. By the time the financial sector reforms of 1992/1993 were implemented, the prevailing view within the MoF was that as long as an applicant met the minimum legal requirements for registration there was no need to consider the convenience and needs of the financial system or economy.

Between 1992 and 1994, the MoF registered a comparatively large number of banks. Using the same expressions documented ten years earlier, senior officials within the MoF called for "care in the future registration of banks in view of the rapid increase in the number of banks in the market." For the first time, senior officials within the MoF referred to the possible failure of some of the banks. Officials made comparisons with Kenya where a mushrooming of banks, was followed by the failure of a number of banks. The officials in the Ministry were concerned that, if they did nothing, the same would happen in Zambia.

Prospects for Profitable Operation of That Business

The Registrar did not conduct any independent financial analysis of the applicant's prospects for profitability. The office of the Registrar did not have the technical know-how to assess the business plans submitted by the applicants. Instead, effective 1992, the Registrar deferred the business plans to the BoZ for its comment. Before then, there is no evidence suggesting that applicants were even required to submit their business plan when applying for a licence. BoZ's evaluation of the business plan was, however, at best, cursory. Although the January 1993 BoZ Bank Inspection Handbook required inspectors to assess prospective business plans for at least a three-year period, there is no evidence of inspectors conducting such analyses.

BANKING LICENSE REFORMS

Introduction

In line with the post-liberalisation banking reforms, the MoF/BoZ introduced important changes to the licensing process. The BFSA, 1994

formed the basis for the new approach to evaluating bank license applications (Table 2).

Minimum Capital Requirements

In August 1994, the FSSD completed a study aimed at revising up-
wards, the minimum capital requirements for opening a bank. The department realized that the then-minimum capital of K20 million required
by the Banking Act was inadequate. The level of K20 million was set
around 1998 when the value of the domestic currency was approximately K11 to US$1 (US$2 million). However, because of the devalua-
tion of the Kwacha, the minimum capital requirement in US dollars had
declined to approximately US$30,000. The amount was far from suffi-
cient for start-up expenses and capital expenditures associated with
starting-up a new bank. In the absence of a local precedence, the department compared the minimum capital requirements in seven neighboring
countries–Botswana, Kenya, Malawi, Namibia, South Africa, Swaziland,
and Zimbabwe–and recommended an amount of K1 billion.

The study arrived at the sum of K1 billion by taking a simple average
of the Kwacha equivalent of the capital requirement in the seven countries (K4451/7 = K636). This simplified approach ignored the differences in size of the financial sectors and economy found in the sample
countries. Nevertheless, the amount of K1 billion was proposed in an
effort to keep the amount as close as possible to the 1988 original
amount of US$2 million or K1.36 billion at 1994 Kwacha equivalent
value.

TABLE 2. Minimum Capital Requirements in Selected Countries in 1994

Country	Minimum Capital requirement	Kwacha Equivalent K'm
Botswana	P1 million or 6% of total assets	248
Kenya	Kshs 75 million	848
Malawi	MK2 million	185
Namibia	NAD 2 million or 12% of a bank's public liability	400
South Africa	SAR10 million	1900
Swaziland	E1 million	190
Zimbabwe	Equivalent of US$1 million	680

Source: BoZ

The Banking and Financial Services Act, 1994

The BFSA, 1994 introduced significant new licensing legislation while enhancing other existing licensing legislation. The following were emphasised in the Act:

1. Registrar: The position of Registrar was transferred from the MoF to the BoZ to consolidate the licensing process under one institution. The FSSD Director was henceforth to act as Registrar for renewable terms of five years. The rationale was to remove the Minister from the burden of having to be involved in every application but reserve him the right to review any decision–if the applicants were dissatisfied with the BoZ's judgement.
2. Bank Ownership: The number of shares was limited to 25%, unless expressly permitted by the BoZ. This was done to minimise the problems arising because of the negative influence of dominant shareholders who had used their influence over the board and management to obtain loans from the bank on concessionary terms and sometimes in excess of his ability to repay leading to illiquidity and insolvency.
3. Bank Control: The BFSA, 1994 expressly prohibited individuals from controlling more than one bank, except in the case of implementing an amalgamation of two or more banks. Directors were also prohibited from being members of more than one bank Board. Regulators were concerned about the problems of conflicts of interest where a person controlled more than one bank. In addition, there were concerns about concentration of financial power and influence.
4. Duration of Licensing Process: A limit of 120 days for the BoZ to decide on the merit of an application was set in order to enhance regulatory efficiency in processing applications.
5. Administrative Procedures: The BFSA, 1994 also introduced numerous administrative changes to the prohibition of unlicensed businesses (Box 2 and Box 3).

Overall the BFSA, 1994 enhanced the level of corporate governance standards in banks by reiterating the importance of the members of the Board of Directors as the highest policy making body of a bank. However, although the licensing provisions in the Act were admirable, they took effect long after the MoF had granted a significant number of licences; the government was, quite literally, "closing the stable doors long after the horse had bolted."

BOX 2. Revised Licence Application Documents for Zambian-Owned Banks

---

An application shall be accompanied by a written statement containing the following information:

1.   Whether the person applying is doing so in his own capacity, as promoter of the financial institution to be established or as an agent on behalf of a principal;

2.   In the case of an agent on behalf of a principal, the written consent of such principal to the submission of the application on behalf of his client;

3.   The proposed name of the institution;

4.   The proposed place in Zambia where the Head Office of this institution is to be situated;

5.   The nature of the particular type of business to be conducted by the financial institution;

6.   The amount of issued share capital with which the institution is to commence business;

7.   Full details of the anticipated shareholding in the institution;

8.   The nature and sufficiency of the financial resources of the applicant or applicants as a source of continuing financial support for the institutions;

9.   Details of the prospective business plan for the institution for the period of three years commencing on the date on which the institution is for the first time provisionally registered as a financial institution;

10. The proposed memorandum of association and articles of association;

11. The proposed organisational structure and full details of how the affairs of the institution will be managed when it is registered as a financial institution;

12. The name of the proposed auditor of the financial institution;

13. The names and curriculum vitae of the persons who will be chief executive officer and other executive offices of the institution when it is registered as a financial institution;

14. The names, curriculum vitae and the principal business of the directors of the institution;

15. With regard to any individual named in 13 and 14 above, details of any criminal records; and

16. The proposed opening date of the institution.

Source: BoZ Inspection Handbook for Financial Institutions (1993)

Post-1995-1997/98 Bank Failure Reforms

No sooner than the Banking and Financial Services Act had been enacted, three banks failed in 1995. Meridien BIAO Bank, then the fourth largest bank in the country, collapsed on 19 May, African Commercial Bank on 17 November and Commerce Bank later within the same month. Despite the efforts of the BoZ to address the problems facing the local banks, the last quarter of 1997 saw yet another crisis emerge. Prudence Bank collapsed on 17 October, followed by Credit Africa Bank on 2 December, Manifold Investment Bank on 5 December and First Merchant Bank on 2 February 1998. Between 1995 and 1997/98, a total number of nine banks failed. Among the causes of the bank failures strongly debated by the public was the quality of the licensing process.

BOX 3. Revised Licence Application Documents for Foreign-Owned Banks

In addition to all the requirements listed in Box 2, the following are required:

1. A letter from the regulatory authorities in the home jurisdiction that the authorities are aware of the application;

2. Information on the type and scope of supervision that apply in its home jurisdiction;

3. Information on the parent company; name, name of jurisdiction of incorporation, date of incorporation and address of principal office;

4. A list of names and addresses of all companies in which the parent or a company associated with it holds more than 10 per cent of the voting stock, including and outline of the main business undertaken by each of them;

5. An organisation chart of the parent bank and its affiliates, with a list of names and titles of the senior officer;

6. A copy of the latest annual report;

7. A copy of the audited financial statements of the parent bank and of the consolidated organisation, i.e., balance sheet, statement of income and expenses, statement of changes in shareholders equity–for the most recent year–i.e., for a period ended not more than 12 months prior to the date of submitting the material.

Source: BoZ Inspection Handbook for Financial Institutions (1993)

In 1998, the BoZ started revising the Bank licensing procedures and introduced additional criteria for assessing the suitability of applicants for a banking licence. In 1999, the FSSD issued a document setting out a revised licensing procedure. The new licensing procedure requires BoZ to ensure that the initial capital of a bank is sufficient to finance start-up expenses, act as a buffer against losses, provide initial funding of loans and investments, generate an initial source of income and to serve as an indicator of the viability and market presence of the bank. The new policy also restricts the admission of non-cash items as capital to 10% of the required level of start-up capital. In addition, the non-cash contributions must be of a kind that would be of sufficient use in the ordinary course of business in a bank. Further, the initial capital should be financed out of the shareholders' own funds, not out of borrowed money. In addition, the 1995 Capital Adequacy Regulations increased the minimum capital requirement to K2 billion.

The vetting process for shareholders now includes consultations with the tax authorities, home country regulators (for foreign banks), and other banks in the country (enquiring on whether the major promoters (1% shares or above) have any non-performing loans with any of the banks.) License applicants are further required to submit; (1) a written statement from a foreign supervisory authority that the shareholder is in good standing and has no history of conflicts with the foreign supervisor; (2) an auditor's statement on the net-worth of the shareholder; (3) copies of tax returns, indicating the income of the shareholder; (4) extracts from the register, showing the other business interests of the shareholder and financial statements with regard to these other interests; (5) police statements that the shareholder has not been investigated/convicted by the police with regard to any criminal activity on the part of the shareholder; (6) court or police affidavits that the shareholder has not been convicted of any substantial crime; and (7) a completed and signed questionnaire by all shareholders.

The applicants must also show that management is "fit and proper" for the offices they have been appointed to. The burden of proof is on the part of the applicant. Fitness and propriety are evaluated by (1) requesting a completed directors form and curriculum vitae of prospective managers; (2) using any legitimate means of its own in collecting information about bank managers, for instance, if a prospective manager has worked for a bank before; (3) conducting an informal discussion with the prospective managers, and if the prospective manager has exercised banking business in another country; (4) obtaining a clearance letter from the supervisory authorities in that country. The list of qualities to be tested include probity (a reputation of honesty, integrity and uprightness), knowledge (of financial matters gained through formal training, with sufficient management expertise), experience, judgement (ability and willingness to make sensible and wise decisions), reputation, character and diligence.

The new guideline does not specify how to assess the convenience and needs of the community. It merely states, "The applicant must convince the Registrar that the proposed bank meets a need and will, therefore, have the support of the community." The applicant must demonstrate that it has a strategy for attracting and maintaining community support for the new bank. The applicant must also demonstrate that the services to be offered will be responsive to those needs, will be convenient to customers, can be provided by the bank profitably, and will be consistent with the safe and sound banking practices. The burden of proof lies with the applicants and not the BoZ.

Assessing the prospects for the profitable operation of that business now requires inspectors to verify whether the relevant externalities have been taken into account in the business plan: assumed development of interest rates, exchange rate, development of certain economic sectors, availability of staff and management, etc. Apart from checking that the business plan is also internally consistent and plausible, a fundamental change to the overall approach is that BoZ will also verify by means of interviews and discussions whether the management of the bank, who will be responsible for the implementation of the plan, fully understand the plan, can discuss it and defend it in a convincing manner. They should be able to explain it to the supervisory authorities in their own words, and without reference to the text. Previously, interviews of this nature were not required. In assessing the application BoZ utilises the profit and loss projections submitted as part of the business plan. Drawing on the experience of existing banks and knowledge of the financial market, the review should then reach a judgment as to whether the profit forecast is reasonable and achievable. This will give the new management an opportunity to demonstrate their professionalism and prudence. Subsequent profit results may then be compared to management's initial forecast as part of the exercise to assess how well managed the bank is.

SUMMARY AND CONCLUSION

In its review of the MoF bank licensing polices in the preceding years of the 1995-1997/8 bank failures, this paper identified significant deficiencies. By focusing on the minimum legally-required capital requirements, the MoF neglected the need for banks to raise sufficient business capital. The source and existence of capital was not thoroughly investigated as the MoF relied on the minimal information provided by the applicants nor was there any third party confirmation. Until 1989, the MoF had no criteria for assessing the character and experience of major shareholders and directors. Later, when applicants' details were referred to the state security department's requests for information often went unanswered or were returned to the MoF late. Bank license applications whose applicants faced criminal investigations continued to be processed until the application was approved. The MoF permitted applicants to replace the 'suspect' concerned without tarnishing the credibility of the entire application. There was no evidence indicating that any of the banks assessed for their potential individual contribution to the convenience and needs of the banking sector or their prospects for financial viability. Finally, there was a high number of former senior BCCI officials that entered the banking sector through the newly-licensed banks, either as owners or managers. The MoF made no formal effort to check whether the former BCCI officials had played a role in the closure of the former international bank.

Despite these findings, the study failed to confirm its hypothesis that weaknesses in the bank licensing policies and procedures were significant contributing factors to the 1995-1997/98 bank failures. The weaknesses noted herein applied to both banks that subsequently failed and those that did not. Nevertheless, to the extent that under a more stringent licensing regime, the MoF might not have approved some of the license applications, the weaknesses in its licensing policies and procedures may have contributed to the bank failures.

The post 1995-1997/98 banking license reforms reflect internationally accepted minimum standards for granting bank licenses. The new guidelines are comparatively exhaustive with respect to the information that applicants must submit to the BoZ. However, what the guidelines do not establish are guidelines for inspectors to use in interpreting the information that applicants provide, especially, with respect to their fitness and probity. To date, there are no universal rules for determining the knowledge, experience, judgement, reputation, character and diligence of bank applicants.

The research into prudential licensing requirements needs to proceed beyond identifying desirable minimum requirements to establishing practical tools and techniques for vetting prospective bank owners/directors. The literature recommends that regulators set sufficiently high minimum capital requirements to create appropriate incentives for sound management, yet, it is inconclusive on the criteria that regulators should use to determine the appropriate level of capital that banks require. There is also consensus in the literature in calling for 'fit and proper' and proper owners/directors. However, there is vagueness, on the suitability of methods for determining fitness and probity. For future research to be useful, it must aid regulators in determination of the level of discretion that regulators should exercise in evaluating bank license applications. While a strict legal interpretation of the minimum legal requirements may preclude the inclusion of other factors that are unique to that bank, an inappropriate amount of regulatory discretion may encourage undesirable rent-seeking behaviour.

For developing countries, the practical arguments on fitness and probity are further complicated by the institutional weakness of the regulatory and supervisory system. The absence of credit rating agencies makes it difficult to ascertain the credit worthiness of applicants. The slow judicial process makes it difficult to obtain swift judicial review of an individual's innocence or guilt with respect to possible investigations into their activities. Finally, the generally inefficient nature of the civil service means that it is difficult to obtain information that may augment the licensing process such as an individual's compliance to domestic tax and business laws.

Regulators must address these institutional weaknesses alongside the on-going legislative reforms, without adopting an overly cautious approach to licensing banks, which may result in a strong bias against the registration of local banks. Despite the fact that all the banks that failed in both the 1995 and 1997/98 period were local banks, it is important that regulators do not discourage their registration. Local banks can provide services that foreign and Government banks are either unwilling or unable to supply, and can also inject the much-needed financial competition in the financial sector. They extend access to individuals and small businesses that experience difficulty in relating with the formal banking sector. Further, unlike foreign banks, they invested in the rural sectors where the latter were either divesting from that market altogether or maintaining, but concentrating on corporate clients. The key to ensuring that local bank failures are avoided is not in discouraging their registration, but rather in ensuring that they are prudently and honestly managed.

REFERENCES

Bank of Zambia (1993). *Bank of Zambia Bank Inspection Handbook*. Lusaka: Bank of Zambia.

Basel Committee on Banking Supervision (1988). *International Convergence of Capital Measurement and Capital Standards*. (Basel: Bank of International Settlements).

Basel Committee on Banking Supervision (1999). *Core Principles Methodology*. (Basel: Bank of International Settlements).

Basel Committee on Banking Supervision (2001). *Capital Adequacy Framework*. (Basel: Bank of International Settlements).

Benston, G. (1992). International Bank Capital Standards. In Peter Gray et al., (Eds.) *Emerging Challenges for the International Financial Services Industry* (pp. 51-73). London: Research in International Business and Finance, (9).

Berger, A. et al. (1995). The Role of Capital in Financial Institutions. *Journal of Banking and Finance*, *19*, 393-430.

Blum, J. and Hellwig, M. (1995). The Macro-economic Implications of Capital Adequacy Requirements for Banks. *European Economic Review*, *39*, 739-749.

Brownbridge, M. (1996). Financial Policies and the Banking System in Zambia. *IDS Working Paper* (32), (University of Sussex).

Brownbridge, M. and Gockel, A. (1996). The Impact of Financial Sector Policies on Banking in Ghana. *IDS Working Paper* (30). (University of Sussex).

Brownbridge, M. and Harvey, C. (1998). *Banking in Africa: The Impact of Financial Sector Reform Since Independence*. Oxford: James Currey.

Calomiris, C. W. (1992). Comment on International Bank Capital Standards. In Peter Gray et al., (Eds.) *Emerging Challenges for the International Financial Services Industry* (pp. 75-81). London: Research in International Business and Finance, (9).

Calomiris, W. (1998). Could Banks Police Each Other? *The Economist*, 17th October 1998 (Economic Focus).

Caprio, G. (1996). Bank Regulation: The Case of the Missing Model. *World Bank Policy Research Working Paper, 1574.*

Classens, S. et al. (1998). How Does Foreign Entry Affect the Domestic Banking Market? *World Bank Policy Research Working Paper, 1918,* (Revised).

Folkerts-Landau, D. and Lindgren, C. (1997). *Toward a Framework for Financial Stability.* Washington D.C.: International Monetary Fund.

Gardner, E. (1979). "Capital Adequacy and Banking Supervision–Towards a Practical System" in Edward Gardner, (Ed.) *UK Banking Supervision: Evolution, Practice and Issues.* Allen & Urwin, London.

Goodhart, C. (1995b). *The Central Bank and the Financial System.* London: Macmillan.

Harvey, C. (1996). The Limited Impact of Financial Sector Reforms in Zimbabwe. *IDS Working Paper (36),* (The University of Sussex).

Harvey, C. (1999). The Impact on Southern Africa of the Financial Crises in Asia and Russia. *BIDPA Working Paper (19),* (Botswana Institute For Development Policy Analysis).

Howard, D. and Hoffman, G. (1980). *Evolving Concepts of Bank Capital Management.* New York: Citicorp.

Jackson, P. et al. (1998). Bank Capital and Value-At-Risk. *Bank of England Working Paper Series (79).*

Jackson et al. (1999). "Capital Requirements and Bank Behaviour: The Impact of the Basle Accord." *Basle Committee on Banking Supervision Working Papers.* No. 1 April 1999. Switzerland: Basel.

Llewellyn, D. (1992). Bank Capital: The Strategic Issues of the 1990's. *Banking World,* (January), 20-25.

Mehran, H. et al. (1998). Financial Sector Development in Sub-Saharan African Countries. *IMF Occasional Paper (169).* Washington D.C.

Polizatto, V. (1990). Prudential Regulation and Banking Supervision: Building and Institutional Framework for Banks. In Phillippe Callier, (Eds.) *Financial Systems and Developments in Africa.* Washington D.C. World Bank.

Revell, J. (1979). Capital Adequacy, Hidden Reserves and Provisions. In Edward Gardner (ed.) *UK Banking Supervision: Evolution, Practice and Issues.* London: Allen and Urwin.

Shah, A. (1996). Why Capital Adequacy Regulation for Banks? *Journal of Financial Regulation and Compliance,* 4(3), 278-290.

Short, B. (1978). "Capital requirements for commercial banks: A survey of the issues." *IMF Staff Papers,* September 1978.

APPENDIX 1

Banks Licensed in Zambia (1906-1994)

No.	Name of Bank	Year of Incorporation
1	*Standard Chartered Bank*	1906
2	Barclays Bank	1918
3	Stanbic Bank	1956
4	Zambia National Commercial Bank	1970
5	Citibank	1979
6	Meridien Bank BIAO*	1984
7	Indo-Zambia Bank	1984
8	African Commercial Bank*	1984
9	Finance Bank	1984
10	Manifold Investment Bank*	1987
11	Zambia Export and Import Bank*	1987
12	Co operative Bank*	1989
13	Commerce Bank*	1989
14	Union Bank*	1991
15	Cavmont Merchant Bank	1992
16	First Alliance Bank	1992
17	New Capital Bank	1992
18	First Merchant Bank*	1992
19	Mercantile Bank*	1993
20	Meridien Financial Services*	1993
21	Ital Bank*	1993
22	Continental Bank*	1993
23	Safe Deposit Bank*	1993
24	Prudence Bank*	1994
25	Credit Africa Bank*	1994
	TOTAL BRANCHES	

Source: BoZ/Note: *: failed banks

Can Prompt Corrective Action Rules Work in the Developing World?

Martin Brownbridge
Samuel Munzele Maimbo

SUMMARY. A major weakness of bank regulation is "regulatory forbearance," which is partly attributable to the scope for discretionary intervention by bank regulators. Therefore, bank regulation might be improved by subjecting intervention policy to a set of rules, such as the "Prompt Corrective Action" (PCA) rules in the US. The introduction of PCA rules is under consideration in a number of developing countries (DCs), stimulated by costly bank failures. This paper examines the potential benefits and feasibility of incorporating PCA rules into banking regulation in DCs. The paper concludes that PCA rules can improve bank regulation in DCs if introduced as part of a comprehensive set of prudential reforms which strengthens the operational independence of the bank regulators, improves their on-site examination capacities,

Martin Brownbridge is Research Associate, Institute for Development Policy and Management, University of Manchester (E-mail: MartinBrownbridge@hotmail.com). Samuel Munzele Maimbo is Financial Analyst, World Bank, Banking and Financial Restructuring Department, Mail stop MC9-907, 1818H Street NW, Washington DC 20433 (E-mail: smaimbo@worldbank.org).

The findings, interpretations and conclusions expressed in this paper are those of the authors alone and do not necessarily represent the views and policies of the World Bank or its Board of Executive Directors or the countries they represent.

[Haworth co-indexing entry note]: "Can Prompt Corrective Action Rules Work in the Developing World?" Brownbridge, Martin, and Samuel Munzele Maimbo. Co-published simultaneously in *Journal of African Business* (International Business Press, an imprint of The Haworth Press, Inc.) Vol. 4, No. 2, 2003, pp. 47-68; and: *African Business Finance and Development Policy* (eds: Victor Murinde and Atsede Woldie) International Business Press, an imprint of The Haworth Press, Inc., 2003, pp. 47-68. Single or multiple copies of this article are available for a fee from The Haworth Document Delivery Service [1-800-HAWORTH, 9:00 a.m. - 5:00 p.m. (EST). E-mail address: docdelivery@haworthpress.com].

strengthens accounting standards and raises public and political understanding of the need for strong and impartial bank regulation. *[Article copies available for a fee from The Haworth Document Delivery Service: 1-800-HAWORTH. E-mail address: <docdelivery@haworthpress.com> Website: <http://www.HaworthPress.com> © 2003 by The Haworth Press, Inc. All rights reserved.]*

KEYWORDS. Prompt corrective action, regulatory forbearance, Zambia

INTRODUCTION

Many developing countries (DCs) implemented reforms to strengthen their banking laws and bank supervision capacities in the 1980s and 1990s. Despite these reforms, widespread bank failures occurred in the 1990s. Although the reforms have improved prudential systems in DCs, key weaknesses remain, one of which is regulatory forbearance. A possible constraint on regulatory forbearance are "Prompt Corrective Action" (PCA) rules of the type enacted in the United States in 1991, which entail a set of public rules, defined in legislation, for determining mandatory intervention by the regulator in distressed banks, including rules for closure. The triggers for regulatory intervention are based on reductions in regulatory capital below pre-specified thresholds. As the objectives of the prudential regulation of banks are to protect deposits and prevent systemic instability in the banking system, the effective implementation of PCA rules should improve bank regulation by forcing the early resolution of distressed banks before their capital is wiped out and depositors and other creditors suffer losses.

The introduction of PCA rules is under consideration in a number of DCs, in part stimulated by bank failures in the 1990s, which proved costly for governments and taxpayers. This paper examines whether introducing PCA rules in DCs can provide an effective constraint on regulatory forbearance, and in doing so, improve bank regulation. It also considers what complementary reforms might be necessary to enable PCA rules to work effectively in DCs. The paper is organised as follows. Section 2 examines why regulatory forbearance is such an important problem for bank regulation, and the consequences of forbearance for the incentive structure facing banks. Section 3 provides empirical evidence of regulatory forbearance. Section 4 outlines the rationale for, and the key features of, PCA rules, and discusses their potential advantages and disadvantages. Section 5 discusses whether the prerequisites for the effective use of PCA rules exist in DCs and also considers what additional reforms are likely to be needed in DCs to complement PCA rules if the latter are to be operationalised effectively. The conclusion of the paper is that PCA rules are not a panacea against regulatory forbearance but can help to improve bank regulation if implemented as part of a broader package of reforms to strengthen prudential systems.

REGULATORY FORBEARANCE

Regulatory forbearance refers to the failure of a bank regulator to enforce prudential regulations and to intervene promptly in distressed banks and take actions, which force the resolution of these banks, without transferring the losses onto taxpayers. Honohan and Klingebiel (2000) distinguish between three degrees of regulatory forbearance. The most accommodating form of forbearance allows banks, which are known by the regulator to be insolvent, to remain open. An intermediate degree of forbearance involves the regulator allowing an undercapitalised bank to remain open under its existing management for an extended period of time, while a less accommodating form of forbearance involves the temporary relaxation or non enforcement of prudential regulations such as loan provisioning rules (Honohan and Klingebiel, 2000: 7).

Regulatory forbearance is the result of a number of factors; legal, political, institutional and economic. Although the banking laws usually provide the regulators with the legal authority to intervene in distressed banks, they often omit to delineate clear rules for when intervention should take place, leaving the decision to intervene to the discretion of the regulators (Glaessner and Mas, 1995).

Regulatory forbearance also reflects a principal-agent problem in bank regulation. Under the banking laws of many countries, bank regulators have a statutory responsibility to protect deposits and the stability of the financial system. Hence the principals of the regulators should be bank depositors and the wider public who benefit from a stable financial system. However, the public are unable to perfectly monitor the actions of their agents, the regulators, because a large part of the operations of bank regulation are not publicly observable. Moreover, in reality bank regulators may have multiple principals, including politicians and powerful business interests who are able to exercise influence over the regulators (Murshed and Subagjo, 2000). The regulators may face political pressure to exercise forbearance, because the owners or debtors of distressed banks are politically influential, or because government fears that bank closures, with the disruption caused to bank customers and the loss of jobs, will be unpopular with the public. Also, the regulators may be reluctant to tackle powerful bank owners or may be "captured" by the banks they are mandated to regulate if, for example, regulators move jobs between the regulatory authority and banks, or are financially compromised by the banks.

Regulatory forbearance has adverse consequences on the incentive structure facing bank owners and managers. The ex-ante expectation that regulators will exercise forbearance in the event that a bank becomes distressed weakens the incentives on bank owners and managers to avoid taking actions, which might lead to the distress of their bank. If a bank is allowed to remain open once it has become insolvent or is close to insolvency, there is acute moral hazard because the owners have no capital left to protect through prudent management. Instead, they have strong incentives to try to recover their lost capital by investing in high-risk assets, knowing that if the strategy is successful they will appropriate the gains by restoring the bank's capital but that if it is unsuccessful all of the losses will be borne by the depositors or taxpayers. This has been termed "gambling for resurrection." The bank's owners may even loot the bank's remaining assets while its staff have incentives to commit fraud if they doubt whether the bank can be salvaged (Akerlof and Romer, 1993).

Whether regulatory forbearance increases moral hazard for depositors (i.e., weakens incentives for them to monitor the banks in which they deposit money) depends upon the nature of the safety net for depositors. If the formal deposit insurance scheme is strictly limited to small depositors, so that most deposits are uninsured, and if there is no implicit insurance of the deposits not covered by the deposit insurance scheme, regulatory forbearance could increase the probability that depositors will suffer losses in failed banks. This is because forbearance will allow the banks to operate for longer in an insolvent state, and thus accumulate larger losses, which will be eventually borne by depositors. Hence a combination of weak prudential regulation and strictly limited deposit insurance would give depositors strong incentives to avoid potentially unsound banks, provided that depositors actually believe that only small deposits would be protected by the government.

However, because of the political consequences of imposing losses on depositors, it is more likely that regulatory forbearance is combined with ex-post de facto insurance of deposits, and ex-ante implicit insurance. This was the case in some of the East Asian countries prior to the financial crisis of 1997/98, where banks had rarely been allowed to fail by the authorities. The combination of regulatory forbearance and implicit insurance for deposits and other bank liabilities creates moral hazard for both the banks and their creditors. Depositors and other creditors have little incentive to monitor the banks in which they invest their money if they believe that the government will bear all of the risk, while the banks can attract funds simply by offering above market interest rates and use these funds for high risk investments. Moreover, by bidding up the cost of deposits, imprudently managed banks can transmit adverse incentives for imprudent management to other banks in the market.

Regulatory forbearance is costly for taxpayers. Honohan and Klingebiel (2000) examined banking crises in 34 countries, the resolution of which, on average, cost the government budget 12% of GDP, in order to determine whether the fiscal costs of the banking crises were related to bank intervention and resolution policies. By regressing the fiscal costs of the banking crises on various measures of government response to the crises, the authors found that lax intervention and resolution policies had a significant and large impact on the fiscal costs. In particular, the provision of liquidity support and of unlimited deposit guarantees, and two indicators of regulatory forbearance–allowing insolvent banks to remain open, and the suspension of prudential regulations–all significantly raised the fiscal cost of the banking crises.

EVIDENCE OF REGULATORY FORBEARANCE FROM ZAMBIA

This section examines intervention in distressed banks in Zambia in the 1990s.[1] The regulator, the Bank of Zambia (BOZ), closed seven banks in 1995 and 1997/98. There was a substantial time lag between the identification of a problem at a bank, and its eventual closure. This delay took two forms. First, there was a delay between the financial distress of a bank first being detected and the confirmation of its undercapitalisation or insolvency. Secondly, there was a subsequent delay between the confirmation of insolvency or undercapitalisation and the closure of the bank by the regulator. In 1995 the second type of delay was relatively short: once the BOZ confirmed insolvency, it closed the insolvent bank within a period of two to three months. The first type of delay occurred because of weaknesses in the supervisory resources and lack of up-to-date financial data on banks that was available to the BOZ. On the other hand, in 1997/98 the second type of delay was more significant; in excess of 12 months. The delays in closing insolvent banks were attributed by some observers to political pressures and to the concerns of the BOZ about potential systemic effects on the banking system in the wake of the 1995 bank failures. In addition, distressed banks continued to receive liquidity support from the BOZ long after it must have been apparent that the banks were in serious difficulties. By the time the BOZ closed each financial distressed bank, they had accumulated significant liabilities to the BOZ and other government institutions.

In the 12 months leading up to each of the bank closures, the BOZ implemented a variety of supervisory actions as provided for under the banking laws. The different supervisory tools and techniques were grouped into three broad activities–information based activities, liquidity mobilisation activities and management intervention activities.

During the first phase, the emphasis was on obtaining additional information about the financial condition of the bank through bank inspections; follow-ups of audit reports, and written requests for clarification or additional information. Any supervisory actions to improve the financial condition of the bank at this stage involved the willing participation of the bank's management. The regulator requested bank reorganization/recapitalisation plans, held meetings with the bank's owners and managers and discussed their plans for improving the bank's financial position. The strongest supervisory actions at this point were Memorandums of Understanding and restrictions on the bank's activities, especially lending activities and/or letters of reprimand for their breach.

The second phase of regulatory actions focused on mobilising financial resources for the distressed bank. At the individual bank level, this involved providing regulatory, accounting and statutory exemptions, which were forms of regulatory forbearance. These included suspending the payment of interest on overdrafts with the BOZ and exempting the distressed banks from implementing loan provisioning requirements and complying with the minimum capital requirements. At the industry level, mobilising financial resources included; agreeing to provide BOZ guarantees on loans from third parties, encouraging private commercial bank financial support and encouraging a sale, merger or acquisition of the distressed bank. Finally, at the government level, financial support commonly involved overdraft facilities from the BOZ and deposits from government ministries, parastatals and pension funds.

The third and last phase involved direct intervention by the regulator in the management of the failing bank. The BOZ typically started by appointing a member of its Supervision Department to monitor the bank on a daily basis. Thereafter, it appointed a resident inspector to monitor as well as authorise all payments and money transfers at the bank. Other actions at this stage included the suspension/removal of the Chairman, Managing Director or other senior managers and/or the appointment of a curator. Once these measures were exhausted, the BOZ closed the bank and appointed a receiver until the bank went into liquidation or, in the case of one bank, reopened.

Although the timing of the implementation of each of these phases during the period leading up to a bank's closure was different for each bank, three general patterns emerged from the study as indicated in Figure 1. First, the information based activities continued throughout the period. There was a constant stream of meetings, exchange of correspondence and bank inspections/special investigations; all of which increased in measure as the rate of financial deterioration progressed.

Secondly, the financial resource mobilisation phase was heavily dependent on the use of the central bank's lender of last resort facility, which the BOZ made available to all of the banks that failed in 1995 and 1997/98. There was a very limited amount of private sector support provided to the failing banks, which indicates that the market perception of the financial viability of these banks cannot have been high.

FIGURE 1. Current Approach to Implementing Supervisory Actions

Supervisory activity	Phase One	Phase Two	Phase Three
Information based activities			
Financial resource mobilisation activities			
Direct central bank intervention stage			

BOZ intervention in the failing banks took place in the last three to four months leading up to the closure of the bank. These interventions included the appointment of a resident bank inspector, changes in the management, and the appointment of a curator. In all cases, direct BOZ intervention occurred after the bank was confirmed to be insolvent.

The objective of PCA rules should be to ensure a quicker progression from information-based activities to direct regulatory intervention in financially distressed banks, as indicated in Figure 2 below.

For banks that have reached the level of financial deterioration that some of the failed banks in Zambia had reached in 1995 and 1997/98, there are diminishing incremental benefits of additional information about the bank. The key to successful crisis management rests in quickly mobilising the required financial resources, by forcing the existing owners to inject more capital or by bringing in new shareholders, and in addressing the managerial problems of the financially distressed bank. If this cannot be done within a limited period of time, the bank should be closed to prevent further losses to its deposits. PCA rules that achieve a quicker and stronger regulatory response will substantially reduce the costs imposed by a bank failure on the failed bank's creditors. It may even be possible to curtail the rate of financial deterioration and restore the bank to financial solvency and liquidity. If there is an improvement in the bank's financial performance then supervisory action can return to information based activities for monitoring purposes as shown by the dotted lines in Figure 2.

FIGURE 2. PCA Rules Based Approach to Supervisory Action

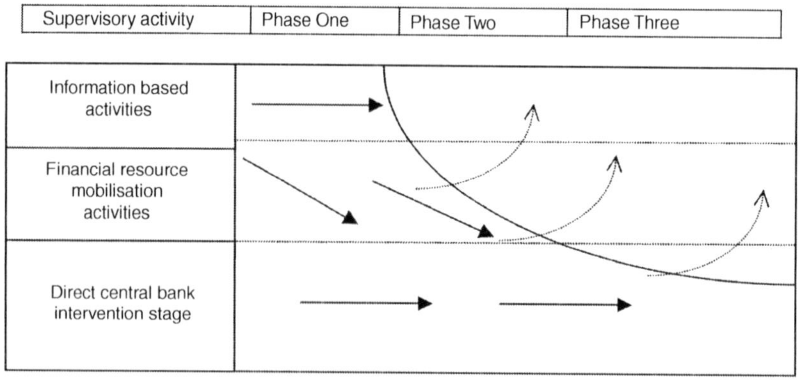

RULES-BASED INTERVENTION POLICY

PCA rules were first introduced in the United States in 1991 as part of the Federal Deposit Insurance Corporation Improvement Act (FDICIA). They were based on the concept of Structured Early Intervention and Resolution developed in the US in the 1980s in response to the widespread failures of Savings and Loans institutions (S & L's), many of which had been granted regulatory forbearance by the regulators. The failures of the S & L's, together with generous deposit insurance, eventually cost US taxpayers around $150 billion (Benston and Kaufman, 1997; Kane, 1989). A weaker version of the PCA rules was introduced in Japan in 1998.

PCA rules aim to limit the discretion of the regulators to intervene in distressed banks, by mandating the regulators to undertake specific interventions on a timely basis, so that the distressed bank is recapitalised or otherwise resolved before its capital is entirely wiped out and losses are incurred by its depositors and other creditors. The PCA rules attempt to mimic the type of remedial actions which private bond holders would impose on debtors in the absence of any government insurance (Goldstein and Turner, 1996: 51).

The triggers for regulatory intervention under the US PCA rules are provided by a bank's capital ratios. The FDICIA defines five capital zones based on three capital ratios: total capital and tier one capital, both as a percentage of risk adjusted assets, plus a tier one leverage ratio. The capital ratios provide thresholds which trigger a set of discretionary and mandatory interventions, involving restrictions on the activities of the bank and specified remedial actions which the bank must take. As capital falls below each threshold, the discretionary and mandatory actions become progressively tougher. For example, when a bank's tier one capital to risk adjusted assets falls below 4%, its total capital to risk adjusted assets falls below 8%, or its tier one leverage ratio falls below 4%, it is deemed undercapitalised and is required to submit and implement a capital restoration plan and must restrict asset growth. Once its tangible equity falls below 2%, when the bank is termed "critically undercapitalised," the regulators must place the bank under receivership or conservatorship within 90 days, and must put it into receivership if it remains critically undercapitalised after four quarters. See Table 1 for a detailed description of the PCA rules in the US. The threshold for closure is set at a low but positive level of measured capital, at which a bank would have a high probability of failure. It is positive, and not zero, because of the difficulties involved in accurately

TABLE 1. Summary of Prompt Corrective Action Provisions of the Federal Deposit Insurance Corporation Improvement Act, 1991

Zone	Capital Ratios (%)			Mandatory Provisions	Discretionary Provisions
	Risk Based		Leverage		
	Tier 1	Tier 2	Tier 1		
1. Well Capitalised	>6	>10	>5		
2. Adequately Capitalised	>4	>8	>4	1. No brokered deposits without FDIC approval	
3. Undercapitalised	<4	<8	<4	1. No brokered deposits 2. Suspend dividends and management fees 3. Require capital restoration plan 4. Restrict asset growth 5. Approval required for acquisitions, branching and new activities	1. Order recapitalisation 2. Restrict inter-affiliate transactions 3. Restrict deposit interest rates 4. Restrict certain other activities 5. Any other action that would better carry out prompt corrective action
4. Significantly Undercapitalised	<3	<6	<3	1. Same as for Zone 3 2. Order recapitalisation* 3. Restrict inter-affiliate transactions* 4. Restrict deposit interest rates* 5. Pay of officers restricted	1. Any Zone 3 discretionary actions 2. Conservatorship or receivership if it fails to submit or implement plan to recapitalise pursuant to order 3. Any other Zone 5 provision if such action is necessary to carry out prompt corrective action
5. Critically Undercapitalised			<2	1. Same as for Zone 4 2. Receivership or conservatorship within 90 days* 3. Receivership if still in Zone 5 after four quarters 4. Suspend payments on subordinated debt* 5. Restrict certain other activities	

* These actions are not required if the primary supervisor determines that they would not serve the purpose of prompt corrective action or if certain other conditions are met

Source: Benston and Kaufman (1997: 147); Goldstein and Turner (1996: 52-53)

measuring the value of a bank's assets relative to the values, which would be realised through the liquidation process (Estrella, Park and Peristiani, 2000).

Figure 3 illustrates the operation of PCA rules. As a bank's capital falls through zones 1 to 5, the regulatory actions taken by the regulator become progressively tougher. A progressively tougher regulatory response, entailing the imposition of tighter prudential controls on the management of the bank together with requirements for recapitalisation, is justified for two reasons. First, as a bank's capital falls, the buffer provided by capital for absorbing losses on its asset portfolio is diminished, increasing the probability that its deposits will be lost. Secondly, as a bank's capital falls, the incentives on the bank's owners for prudent management decline, further increasing the probability that losses will occur which will erode its deposits. The PCA rules are intended to ensure that if the decline in a bank's capital cannot be halted and reversed, the bank is resolved before its deposits and other liabilities are lost.

The FDICIA also includes Least Cost Resolution (LCR) provisions that complement the PCA rules by mandating the regulators to resolve an intervened bank in a manner, which imposes the lowest costs on the deposit insurance fund. This requirement can be suspended in cases where LCR would have adverse economic consequences or pose systemic risks to the financial system (e.g., where a bank is deemed "too big to fail"), although there are stringent conditions attached to the use of this exemption.

FIGURE 3. Regulatory Response to Capital Deterioration

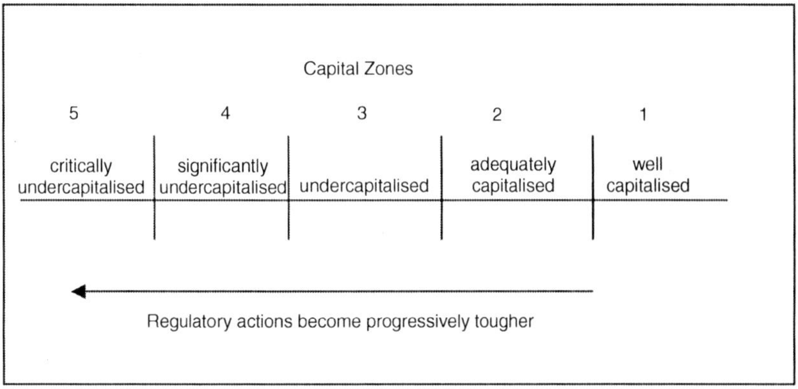

Have PCA Rules Improved Bank Regulation in the United States?

The bank regulators in the United States resisted the PCA rules, and the rules enacted in the FDICIA were a weakened version of those initially proposed to Congress.[2] Despite this, PCA appears to have improved bank regulation and bank soundness in the US. Benston and Kaufman (1977) argue that the enactment of FDICIA has brought about three important benefits. First, the regulators have intervened more promptly in under-capitalised banks, albeit not as promptly in all cases as the regulations require. Secondly, the banking industry has been encouraged to raise additional capital in order to more than meet the minimum capital ratios required by the banking laws and thus reduce the risk of being subject to regulatory intervention. Thirdly, the Federal Deposit Insurance Corporation has reduced markedly the extent to which it protects the uninsured deposits of large insolvent financial institutions during the resolution process. Aggarwal and Jacques (1998), using econometric tests, found that the introduction of the PCA rules induced banks to increase their capital ratios, and also induced both adequately capitalised and undercapitalised banks to reduce their level of asset portfolio risk.

Jones and King (1995) are more skeptical of the efficacy of PCA. They present research showing that risk-based capital ratios, which provide the triggers for regulatory intervention, were poor indicators of insolvency risk in the period 1984-89, which was before the enactment of FDICIA. Their research indicates that the majority of troubled or high-risk banks in this period would not have been categorized as undercapitalised using risk-based capital ratios and, therefore, would not have been subject to mandatory regulatory actions had the PCA rules been in-force at that time. However, Estrella, Park and Peristiani (2000), using US banking data from the period 1988-93, found that capital ratios were good predictors of subsequent bank failure, even over a two- to three-year period prior to a bank closure.

Potential Advantages and Drawbacks of a Rules-Based Intervention Policy

There are several channels through which a rules-based intervention policy, such as PCA, could improve bank regulation, especially by strengthening the incentives facing the bank regulators as well as bank owners and managers. The objective of PCA rules is to force the regulators to intervene earlier and more effectively in distressed banks. Earlier intervention by the regulators will improve the chances that distressed banks can be either successfully rehabilitated or closed before depositors and other creditors have suffered losses.

As noted in section 2 above, among the causes of inefficient bank regulation are principal-agent problems, arising because the regulators have multiple principals. By clearly delineating the responsibilities of the regulators to intervene in problem banks, PCA rules restrict regulatory discretion and can thereby help to mitigate principal-agent problems. The PCA rules can help to ensure that the regulators act in the interests of the principals whom they are mandated by law to serve–the depositors and wider public–and not to act in the interests of others, such as politicians and bank owners, who are in a position to influence the regulators. In addition, the PCA rules should provide the regulators with some protection against political pressure to exercise forbearance, because the regulators will be able to point out to politicians that the law mandates them to intervene in problem banks.

To the extent that PCA rules strengthen the incentives facing the regulators to intervene in problem banks, this will also improve the incentives facing bank owners and managers to exercise prudent bank management, because it will reduce the expectation, held by bank owners and managers, that the regulators will extend forbearance to a distressed bank. This will discourage banks from undertaking risks, which might deplete their capital and trigger intervention by the regulators and should also enhance the incentives on banks to maintain higher levels of capital.

A rules-based intervention policy can also help to avoid the time inconsistent characteristics of a discretionary intervention policy. A discretionary intervention policy, like other discretionary policies such as monetary policy, may be time inconsistent and socially sub-optimal because of its impact on the private sector's expectations and decision making. Ex-ante, it is optimal for the regulators to signal that insolvent banks will be closed, to maximise incentives on the banks for prudent management. Ex-post, after a bank has failed, it may not be socially or politically optimal for the government to close the insolvent bank. Hence a discretionary intervention policy may lack credibility because the banks anticipate that the regulators will not enforce closures, which in turn undermines the incentives for prudent management. In contrast, a rules based intervention policy could carry greater credibility with the banks and the public.

However, by itself a rules based policy is not necessarily credible if the private sector believes that the rules are incentive incompatible (i.e., incompatible with the incentives facing the regulator) and, therefore, will not be enforced by the regulator. Moreover, a rules based policy will not be necessary if the regulator can establish its credibility through some other institutional mechanism (a commitment technology) which would convince the private sector that regulatory forbearance will not be exercised, although it is not clear what sort of commitment technology might be feasible.

The biggest drawback of a rules based intervention policy is the difficulty of applying it fully in cases of systemic banking crises. In many countries there will be banks which are regarded by the regulators as "too big to fail" because their failure would pose a systemic risk to the financial system. The closure of a large bank might also involve the loss of nationwide banking services, which is regarded as socially or politically unacceptable. If some banks are "too big to fail," they cannot be fully subject to the PCA rules, because they cannot be closed, although they could still be subject to other provisions of the PCA rules, such as restrictions on asset growth and payment of dividends. The PCA rules will then be perceived as unfair by smaller banks. In addition, a large macroeconomic shock which adversely affects the loan portfolios of many banks at the same time might also create a potential systemic risk to the banking system in which the enforcement of a rules based closure policy might not be socially optimal (Brock, 2000). In such circumstances, the government might have to provide support to the distressed banks in order to avoid a serious contraction of the banking system.

One possible solution to the problems posed by situations of systemic risk is to include a clause in the PCA rules allowing regulators the discretion to exempt banks from the closure requirements in cases where this would pose a systemic risk, but with explicit conditions attached to the use of any exemption clause. Possible safeguards could include a requirement that the regulators should have to obtain ex-ante approval for their use of the exemption from an independent oversight body and to provide it with a detailed ex-post evaluation of the decision.

Enoch, Stella and Khamis (1997) argue that ambiguity and discretion are preferable to the inconsistent application of clear intervention rules. Because of the heterogeneity of different cases of bank distress, a regulatory response determined on a case by case basis will be more efficient than one based on predetermined rules. In some cases, public support for a distressed bank is justified, but it is not optimal to specify in advance the circumstances under which such support will be provided because of the consequences for moral hazard. Moreover, regulators often will not have sufficient information, such as information about the true capital position of a distressed bank, to justify the implementation of intervention rules. Enoch, Stella and Khamis argue that operational discretion granted to the regulators should be balanced by a requirement for ex-post transparency, involving firm rules for substantive and meaningful public disclosure of the regulators' action after the event.

REQUIREMENTS FOR PCA RULES TO WORK IN DEVELOPING COUNTRIES

The PCA rules were introduced in an economy, that of the US, whose institutional and structural characteristics differ greatly from those found in most DCs. Therefore, whatever the perceived benefits of PCA rules in the US, it does not follow automatically that their adoption in DCs would be equally appropriate. This section examines the preconditions for the successful application of PCA rules, whether such preconditions exist in DCs, and what sort of additional reforms to the prudential systems in DCs might be needed to enable PCA rules to work effectively.

Informational Requirements

PCA rules require clear and observable trigger indicators for regulatory intervention. These triggers are a bank's capital ratios; hence the accurate and timely reporting of banks' balance sheet information to the regulators is needed to operationalise PCA. A bank's capital ratios depend crucially on its accounting policies. The failure to make appropriate provisions for non performing assets and to suspend the accrual to income of unpaid interest inflates a bank's capital. This is often a pervasive problem in DCs, either because the banking regulations don't stipulate strict enough asset classification and provisioning rules, or because the banks fail to comply with the rules. In some cases, what is recorded as paid up capital by a bank may itself have been bought using loans from the same bank. In such circumstances, a bank's reported capital asset ratio is not a reliable indicator of its financial condition, and may convey no meaningful information at all. Even audited financial statements may grossly misrepresent the true capital position of a bank.

Although many DCs have recently strengthened their asset classification and provisioning rules, bringing them into line with international best practise, enforcement of these rules will remain problematic because accounting standards and auditing capacities are often very weak. Nevertheless, there are measures which the regulators can take to improve the accuracy of banks' financial data and thereby increase the value of capital ratios as a trigger for regulatory action.

First, the banking regulations should make compliance with international standards of asset classification, provisioning and income recognition mandatory for banks. Secondly, the regulators should impose meaningful penalties on banks which fail to comply with these mandatory standards, and on their auditors. Thirdly, the regulators should be selective in allowing only reputable and competent accounting firms to audit banks. Fourthly, the regulators must build the capacity to conduct regular on-site examinations of all potential problem banks, because distressed banks have strong incentives to conceal losses from their auditors and the regulators. Although losses can also be concealed from bank examiners, on-site examinations by competent examiners add value to off-site reports and audited financial statements because they provide the regulator with an independent source of information on the banks they regulate. In addition, on-site examinations give the regulators the opportunity to verify the accuracy of the monthly or quarterly financial returns submitted to them by the banks, and so encourage the banks to submit more accurate returns.

The operational effectiveness of PCA rules could be further strengthened by using liquidity indicators to back-up capital ratios as triggers for regulatory intervention. Liquidity has the advantage of being easier for the regulator to monitor than capital: the regulator can know with certainty how much each bank has borrowed from the Central Bank.[3] Although liquidity shortages in a bank are not correlated perfectly with its capital, it is usually the case that highly illiquid banks are insolvent, although the obverse is not always the case: insolvent banks are not always illiquid. Consequently a bank with reported capital ratios which are above the intervention thresholds, but which borrows heavily from the Central Bank, should warrant at least the first stages of the graduated mandatory intervention specified in the PCA rules. This should also trigger closer monitoring by the regulators including an on-site inspection. The failure to improve liquidity within a specified period or the discovering of capital impairment of the bank would then trigger the next stages of regulatory intervention. In Indonesia, in February 1998, the regulatory authority intervened in 54 banks selected using a liquidity criterion because the information needed by the regulators to evaluate the banks' solvency was not available (Enoch, 2000).[4]

Operational Independence of the Regulators

PCA rules will not be effective unless the banking or other relevant legislation clearly confers on the regulators operational independence from government and provides them with the necessary legal authority to carry-out all of the discretionary and mandatory interventions specified in the PCA rules. Legislation should clearly state that the regulators should act independently and not take instructions from any other person or institution in carrying out all of their regulatory functions.

The banking law should give the regulators the explicit legal authority to impose regulatory orders, such as cease and desist orders, on banks and provide for strong penalties when banks fail to comply with these orders. It must also give the regulators explicit authority to take over a bank, to remove its management, to suspend shareholders' rights, to close it and to put it into liquidation, based on the regulators' assessment of that bank's net worth. The regulators must have the legal authority to close and resolve an undercapitalised bank even if its regulatory capital is still positive, provided that this is in the best interests of its depositors. The banking law should grant the regulators immunity from legal action in carrying out their statutory duties, provided that the regulators have acted in "good faith."

The extent to which the banking laws in DCs already include provisions of this nature varies, but in many countries the regulators do not have legal independence and their legal authority to intervene in banks is inadequate. In a survey of the supervisory framework in 18 African countries and the two CFA Franc monetary zones, Mehran et al. (1998), found that the regulators had full autonomy in only eight countries. The regulators' autonomy was rated as average in four countries and the two common monetary zones and was rated as low, partial or limited in six other countries. Moreover, Mehran et al. rated the possibility of the government overruling the regulators as likely in 11 countries and the two common monetary zones. Consequently, if DCs were to introduce PCA rules into their banking laws, in many countries this would have to be accompanied by more wide-ranging institutional reforms to strengthen the operational independence of the regulators.

Enforcement of Sanctions on Management

All regulatory directives under the PCA rules should have agreed deadlines for compliance, with specified penalties and sanctions for non-compliance. Penalties for non-compliance with regulatory directives, such as restrictions on asset growth, should be enforced on individual managers and directors, because unless sanctions personally affect the managers responsible for non-compliance, the incentives for non-compliance remain high. Financial penalties imposed on the bank itself are usually ineffective because they worsen the financial condition of an already financially fragile bank, and are sometimes charged to the Central Bank overdraft facility, so that the Central Bank bears the cost of managerial non-compliance.

Willingness of the Regulators to Enforce PCA Rules

Legislative changes do not by themselves make public bureaucracies function better. Even where regulators are legally independent, they may be reluctant to act against the wishes of powerful figures in the government or in society at large. Informal pressure from government may be equally as effective in preventing the regulators from taking prompt corrective actions as formal constraints, such as the requirement to seek the consent of the Finance Minister before a bank is intervened. In countries where the appointment of public officials is politicised and where their job security is weak, it is unrealistic to expect that the regulators can be totally insulated from political pressure, whatever their legal independence. Poorly paid bank regulators will also be vulnerable to corruption from the banks they regulate. Consequently, the remuneration of bank regulators must be competitive with remuneration in the banking industry.

There are reforms which could help to protect the regulators from political interference and to enhance the incentives on them to enforce the PCA rules. The PCA rules themselves, because they are part of the law, can strengthen the hand of the regulators to resist political pressure, because they can point out to those advocating forbearance that this would violate the law. However, legal restraints alone will not prevent forbearance if the regulators are not held accountable for their actions. Kane (1997) argues that the costs of regulatory forbearance must be made observable to taxpayers if regulatory performance is to improve, so that regulators can be disciplined in the press and the employment market. The accountability of the regulators to the public could be improved if they had to report regularly to an independent oversight body on all of the decisions they took during the preceding period, with justifications for these decisions and a detailed report of their compliance with the PCA rules. The independent body mandated with oversight of the regulators should have the authority to censure them and should make its reports available to the public.

Political Acceptance of the Need for Prudential Intervention

Even if PCA rules are enacted into law, regulators will not be able to enforce them unless there is political and public understanding of the duties of the regulator to intervene in a distressed bank and to close it down on prudential grounds, irrespective of the perceived rights of its shareholders.

Political and public understanding of bank regulatory issues is often weak and intervention in a distressed bank is sometimes perceived as unfair expropriation of the rights of its shareholders. In Uganda, a large bank, partly owned by the cooperative movement, was closed by the regulators several months after it was discovered to be massively insolvent by both an on-site inspection and by the bank's own auditors. Following the bank closure, a Committee of Parliament questioned the decision of the regulator to close the bank, disputed that it was insolvent based on claims made by the owners and recommended that the shareholders be given more time to raise new capital.[5] It is possible that political acceptance of the need for strong prudential regulation and the closure of insolvent banks will only be forthcoming once banks have failed and inflicted substantial losses on their depositors and taxpayers.

CONCLUSION

Regulatory forbearance is a critical weakness in prudential regulation in many DCs. PCA rules are designed to circumscribe the discretion of regulators to exercise forbearance by mandating prompt and graduated interventions in distressed banks based on a progressive worsening of their capital ratios. This is intended to enable the regulators to resolve distressed banks by forcing their recapitalisation or closure before their net worth has been completely wiped out and losses are inflicted on depositors and taxpayers.

There are constraints to the effective implementation of PCA rules in DCs. The regulators often do not have timely and accurate financial data at their disposal because accounting standards are poor and because distressed banks have strong incentives to conceal losses incurred in their asset portfolios. The implementation of PCA rules could also be impeded because the regulators lack adequate legal autonomy from government or face informal pressures from politicians and bankers to exercise forbearance.

Despite these constraints, the introduction of PCA rules into the banking laws of DCs can bring positive benefits. Because the law will mandate regulatory intervention, PCA rules should improve incentives on the regulators to act more promptly to tackle problems in distressed banks, and provide the regulators with some protection against pressure for regulatory forbearance from politicians and bankers. Because they reduce the scope for discretion by the regulators, the PCA rules should also improve the credibility of regulatory policy, although it may take time, and several cases of intervention for the regulators to convince the banking industry that the rules will be strictly enforced. A more credible regulatory policy will improve the incentives on banks for more prudent management.

Given the weaknesses in prudential systems noted above, PCA rules should be introduced as part of a broader package of prudential reforms in DCs. Regulators need more accurate information from banks to operationalise PCA rules. Regulations covering asset classification, provisioning and income recognition should be brought into line with international standards, and meaningful penalties imposed on banks and their auditors, which fail to comply with the regulations. The regulators should also strengthen their capacity for on-site inspections, and focus their scarce inspection capacity on potential problem banks.

Because distressed banks have incentives to conceal losses and mis-report their capital position in their financial returns, indicators of financial distress, which can be monitored more readily, such as illiquidity, should also be used by the regulators as triggers for regulatory intervention, alongside capital ratios. The legal autonomy of the regulators should be set out in law alongside explicit legal authority for the regulators to intervene in banks to protect the interests of depositors. To improve the accountability of the regulators and to strengthen the incentives on them to enforce PCA rules, the regulators should be required to report formally on a regular basis to an independent oversight body, which should evaluate the performance of the regulators and their compliance with the intervention rules.

NOTES

1. The analysis in this section is based on a study of Bank of Zambia documents, including off and on-site reports, financial statements and interviews with regulators and bank officials in Zambia.

2. The PCA rules were resisted by the bank regulators because they perceived the rules as reducing their discretionary powers and their ability to micromanage banks (Benston and Kaufman, 1997: 146).

3. A related issue is the use of lender of last resort (LOLR) facilities. In some countries these facilities have been used to prop up insolvent or undercapitalised banks and this has raised the overall cost of bank failures. The regulators should establish clear rules on the use of LOLR facilities, with use of these facilities above pre-specified thresholds triggering regulatory intervention. At the least, borrowing by a bank from the LOLR facility for longer than a pre-specified maximum period or by more than a maximum amount should trigger an on-site inspection by the regulator to determine the financial condition of the borrowing bank.

4. The criteria used to determine which banks should be brought under the Indonesian Bank Restructuring Agency were that a bank should have a capital asset ratio of below 5% and have borrowed from the Central Bank at least twice its capital (Enoch, 2000: 8).

5. Parliamentary concern about the closure of the Cooperative Bank, and that of other banks, led to the setting up of a Judicial Commission of Enquiry, which subsequently concluded that the regulators' actions in closing and resolving the Cooperative Bank were fully justified.

REFERENCES

Aggarwal, Raj and Kevin T. Jacques (1998). Assessing the Impact of Prompt Corrective Action on Bank Capital and Risk. *Federal Reserve Bank of New York Economic Policy Review* 4 (3): 23-31.

Akerlof, George A. and Paul M. Romer (1993). Looting: The Economic Underworld of Bankruptcy for Profit. *Brookings Papers on Economic Activity* 2: 1-60.

Benston, George J. and George G. Kaufman (1997). FDICIA After Five Years. *Journal of Economic Perspectives* 11 (3): 139-158.

Brock, Philip L. (2000). Financial Safety Nets: Lessons from Chile. *The World Bank Research Observer* 15 (1): 69-84.

Boot, Arnoud W. A. and Anjan V. Thakor (1993). Self-Interested Bank Regulation. *American Economic Review* 83 (2): 206-212.

Caprio, Gerard, Jr. and Patrick Honohan (1999). Beyond Supervised Capital Requirements. *Policy Research Working Paper* 2235, The World Bank.

Dewatripont, Mathias and Jean Tirole (1994). *The Prudential Regulation of Banks*, MIT Press, Cambridge MA.

Enoch, Charles (2000). Interventions in Banks During Banking Crises: The Experience of Indonesia. *Policy Discussion Paper* PDP/00/2, International Monetary Fund.

Enoch, Charles, Peter Stella and May Khamis (1997). Transparency and Ambiguity in Central Bank Safety Net Operations. *Working Paper* WP/97/138, International Monetary Fund.

Estrella Arturo, Sangkyun Park, and Stavros Peristiani (2000). Capital Ratios as Predictors of Bank Failure. *Federal Reserve Bank of New York Economic Policy Review* 6 (2): 33-52.

Glaessner, Thomas and Ignacio Mas (1995) Incentives and the Resolution of Bank Distress. *The World Bank Research Observer* 10 (1): 53-73.

Goldstein, Morris and Philip Turner (1996). Banking Crises in Emerging Economies: Origins and Policy Options. *BIS Economic Papers* 46, Bank for International Settlements.

Honohan, Patrick and Daniela Klingebiel (2000). Controlling the Fiscal Costs of Banking Crises. *Working Paper* 2441, The World Bank.

Jones, David S. and Kathleen Kuester King (1995). The implementation of prompt corrective action: An assessment. *Journal of Banking and Finance* 19: 491-510.

Kane, Edward J. (1989). The High Cost of Incompletely Funding the DSLIC Shortage of Explicit Capital. *Journal of Economic Perspectives* 3 (4): 31-47.

Kane, Edward J. (1997). Comment on 'Understanding Financial Crises: A Developing Country Perspective,' by Frederic S. Mishkin. *Annual World Bank Conference on Development Economics 1996*, The World Bank: 69-75.

Lindgren, Carl-Johan, Tomas J. T. Balino, Charles Enoch, Anne-Marie Gulde, Marc Quintyn and Leslie Teo (1999). Financial Sector Crisis and Restructuring: Lessons from Asia. *Occasional Paper* 188, International Monetary Fund.

Maimbo, Samuel Munzele (2000). The Prediction and Diagnosis of Bank Failures in Zambia. *Finance and Development Research Programme Working Paper* 13, IDPM, University of Manchester.

Mehran, Hassanali, Piero Ugolini, Jean Philippe Briffaux, George Iden, Tonny Lybek, Stephen Swaray, and Peter Hayward (1998). Financial Sector Developments in Sub-Saharan African Countries. *Occasional Paper* 169, International Monetary Fund.

Murshed, S Mansoob and Djono Subagjo (2000). Prudential Regulation in Less Developed Economies. Paper presented at the Development and Business Finance: Policy and Experience in Developing Countries Conference, 5-6 April, Manchester.

Williamson, John and Molly Mahar (1998). A Survey of Financial Liberalization. *Essays in International Finance*, 211, Princeton NJ: Department of Economics, Princeton University.

Nigerian Banks–Quality of Services

Atsede Woldie

SUMMARY. The qualitative characteristics of the service are becoming increasingly important. Quality improvements can lead to increased revenues and decreased costs as a result of increased customer loyalty and the cross-selling of bank products, as loyal customers spend more with chosen banks, attract lower administration costs and are more profitable. The objective of this research is to identify customers' expectations and perceptions of bank service quality to determine the service quality level. It also aims to determine key factors in selecting a particular bank. The findings of the research suggest that the key factors in selecting a particular bank are credibility, location and range of services. The majority of respondents are dissatisfied with the quality of services provided by banks in Nigeria. The research has indicated that complicated procedures and forms, queuing time, lack of individual approach and absence of new technology are some of the factors which create dissatisfaction and lack of co-operation between firms and banks. Interestingly these results are similar to customers in developed countries as indicated by similar studies in developed countries. *[Article copies available for a fee from The Haworth Document Delivery Service: 1-800-HAWORTH. E-mail address: <docdelivery@haworthpress.com> Website: <http://www.HaworthPress. com> © 2003 by The Haworth Press, Inc. All rights reserved.]*

KEYWORDS. Service quality, Nigerian banks

Dr. Atsede Woldie is Senior Lecturer, Glamorgan Business School, University of Glamorgan.

[Haworth co-indexing entry note]: "Nigerian Banks–Quality of Services." Woldie, Atsede. Co-published simultaneously in *Journal of African Business* (International Business Press, an imprint of The Haworth Press, Inc.) Vol. 4, No. 2, 2003, pp. 69-87; and: *African Business Finance and Development Policy* (eds: Victor Murinde and Atsede Woldie) International Business Press, an imprint of The Haworth Press, Inc., 2003, pp. 69-87. Single or multiple copies of this article are available for a fee from The Haworth Document Delivery Service [1-800-HAWORTH, 9:00 a.m. - 5:00 p.m. (EST). E-mail address: docdelivery@haworthpress.com].

INTRODUCTION

The financial sector, and particularly the banking system, plays a very important role in the process of economic development. Banks are the most important and vital financial intermediaries in any economy. They mobilise savings and idle funds from surplus economic units and transfer them to the deficit economic units, who can make better and fuller use of them (Chachi 1989).

Service quality should be an important component of any bank's strategy in creating value and increasing profit. The need for service quality will increase with continuing intensified competition, government legislation, and the growth of technology and increased awareness of consumers.

This study examines organisations' perceptions of the level of service quality provided by Commercial Banks in Nigeria. It also identifies the factors that influence the choice of a particular bank by organisations in Nigeria. The literature has suggested that service quality is of major importance in banking and this has been used as a basis for developing a questionnaire to compare the reasons for choosing the particular bank. It is important that firms should be well informed about what types of services are provided by banks, and whether or not these services are meeting expected standards. Finally, no previous attempts to address the issue of service quality provided by Commercial Banks in Nigeria, after extensive searching of the literature, could be discovered.

BANKING IN NIGERIA

Commercial banking activities started in Nigeria in 1872 with the establishment of the African Banking Corporation, by the British Treasury. Two years later, in 1894, the Bank of British West Africa (now First Bank of Nigeria) was established and it took over the African Banking Corporation. The next commercial bank to appear was Barclays Bank Dominion, Colonial and Overseas (now Union Bank of Nigeria) in 1917.

These banks were set up to provide banking services for the British commercial interests and colonial administration in Nigeria. When the West Africa Currency Board was formed in 1912, the Bank of British West Africa became its agent.

The evolution of banking activities in Nigeria can be classified under five major periods.

THE FREE BANKING ERA (1892-1952)

The Free banking era could be characterised by the following features:

  i. An absence of banking legislation. Anybody could set up a bank provided it is registered under the companies' ordinance.
 ii. The establishment of the three biggest foreign banks (i.e., the bank of British West Africa (1894), the Barclays Bank Dominion, Colonial and Overseas (1917), and the British and French Bank (1948) now called the United Bank for Africa since 1961); and the two biggest indigenous banks: the National Bank of Nigeria (1933), and the African Continental Bank (1947).
iii. An indigenous banking boom. Between 1947 and 1952 alone 185 banking companies registered for business in Nigeria, although most of them collapsed or were declared bankrupt by the government. The uncertainty and loss of confidence resulting from bank failures led to the setting up of the Paton Commission in 1948 to 'enquire into the business of banking in Nigeria and make recommendations to the government on the form and extent of control, which should be introduced.'

THE SECOND PHASE:
PRE CENTRAL BANKING ERA 1952-1959

The main events of the period could be summarised into five parts. The banking ordinance 1952 dealt with the definition of banking, the issuing of banking licence by the financial secretary, the minimum authorised share capital necessary to carry out banking activities, the need to maintain a reserve fund by banks, liquidity requirements, as well as bank examination and supervision.

  i. The collapse of the indigenous banking boom. By the time the ordinance became operational for all banks in the country, 1955, all the indigenous banks, except three: the African Continental Bank, the Agbonmagbe Bank, and the Merchants' Bank, plus the National Bank, which was established in 1933; established since 1945 had collapsed.
 ii. The third feature of this same period is the beginning of state support, or rather, regional government support for and assis-

tance to indigenous banking. Regional self-rule was allowed by the colonial government in 1954. The four indigenous banks which survived the boom could not have done so but for state support and assistance. The Western Region Government injected public funds into the National Bank, the Merchants' Bank, and the Agbonmagbe Bank, while the Eastern Region Government did the same to the African Continental Bank.

The final characteristic of this second phase in commercial banking development in Nigeria was the absence of a central bank. The banking ordinance 1952, was the first ever banking legislation. The ordinance merely sought to provide support for the banks with the lender of last resort facilities; it did not provide investable money market assets; there were no treasury bills, treasury certificates, no commercial bills and no bonds.

THE THIRD PHASE:
ERA OF BANKING LEGISLATION 1959-1970

This period started with the establishment of the Central Bank of Nigeria, in 1959. It can be regarded as a watershed in the annals of Nigeria, because not only was the Nigerian money and capital market established in that year; but also the Treasury Bail Ordinance (1959), the Lagos Stock Exchange (1961) and the Investment Company of Nigeria Act (1959). The latter established the first development finance institution in the country; 1959 was the year when the first public issue of shares and the first Federal Government development loan stock were issued.

Another feature of this period is that a new breed of banks, the mixed banks, emerged in the banking environment.

THE FOURTH PHASE:
THE ERA OF INDIGENISATION 1970-1976

With the Banking Ordinance of 1952-59 laying the legislative background and foundation, the amendments of 1961-64 plugging the observed loopholes and deficiencies in the system, and the banking Decree (1969) consolidating and improving on previous legislation, Nigerian banking was poised for a take-off in the 1970s.

During the period 1970-76, Nigerian banking witnessed three main developments: the indigenisation of Nigerian banking; the renewed boom in indigenous banking; and setting up of the financial system review committee by the Federal Government–known as the Okigbo committee. The Okigbo committee was established in April and it reported in December 1976. This fourth phase brought about major changes in the workings of the Nigeria financial system.

THE FIFTH PHASE:
THE POST-OKIGBO ERA, 1977 ONWARDS

The period started with the release of the government white paper on the Okigbo Report. The white paper gave an indication of the wide-ranging recommendations which the committee made in order to streamline the structure and improve the operations of the commercial banks in particular, and the entire financial system in general.

The government rejected the committee's central recommendation with respect to the commercial banks regarding the establishment of a state bank in each state and the amalgamation of the three biggest indigenous banks into one entity. The Okigbo Report and the White paper on it nevertheless marked a new era in the evolution of the Nigerian financial system in general and Nigerian commercial banking in particular.

LICENSING OF BANKS

The Banking Decree of 1969 stipulates that no banking business shall be transacted in Nigeria except by a company duly incorporated in Nigeria which is in possession of a valid license granted by the commissioner (minister) of Finance authorising it to do so.

The prohibition, however, does not apply to banks duly incorporated under the Banking Act 1958. Any person who transacts banking business without a valid license shall be guilty of an offence and liable to a fine of 100 naira for each day during which the offence continues.

A remarkable feature in the Decree on how banks can be established is that only corporate bodies can set up banks. There is no room for private individuals. Moreover, the Decree applies throughout the country. The minimum paid up capital in respect of a bank which is not directly or indirectly controlled from abroad shall not be less than 600,000 naira, while a bank directly or indirectly controlled from outside the country shall not be less than 1.5 million.

On the question of bank mergers, the Decree provides that every licensed bank must inform the commissioner of finance through the central Bank of Nigeria of any proposed agreement, or arrangement, for any sale or disposal of its business by amalgamation or otherwise.

The commissioner may on the recommendation of the central Bank of Nigeria approve or withhold approval of such merger or take-over bid.

RURAL BANKING IN NIGERIA

The Financial system review committee headed by Dr Pius Okigbo was established in 1976 and a government white paper, established the same year; which assisted the commercial banks to extend their tentacles to reach the rural population.

The Rural banking programme of the Central Bank of Nigeria was established in June 1977. Prior to this Nigeria was grossly underbanked, with one bank serving 137,000 people. Densities in the more developed countries were: United Kingdom 1:4,000; USA 1:6,000; India 1:52,000; Canada 1:3,283 and Japan 1:14,500. Many factors were responsible for the low density in Nigeria, for example the colonial heritage and complacently another nonchalant behaviour of those who have been entrusted with the realms of power and monetary policy and authority since independence.

With over 80 per cent of the population in the rural areas, the financial system never actually penetrated into the normal economic activities of the nation. Soyode and Oyejide in 1973-74 discovered that banks were highly concentrated in the urban areas of Lagos, Kaduna, Enugu, Ibadan and Port Harcourt and that this adversity affected the effective mobilisation of financial resources in the economy.

Until the programme commenced, commercial banks decided for themselves where to open branches. Subsequently, the Central Bank mounted pressures on the banks to open branches in prescribed areas.

The Central Bank also encouraged the establishment of more banking institutions to provide support for small businesses and promote competition in banking.

The inauguration of the rural banking scheme in 1977 resulted in commercial banks, being directed, to open a total of 200 rural branches during the first phase 1977-80. The Central Bank took into consideration, the population, the level of economic activities and the number of established institutions: schools, hospitals, government offices, small business, industries, etc., in deciding the location of branches. The major commercial banks which had previously concentrated their operations in the urban centres were also allocated more branches in the rural areas.

The success of the first phase prompted the launching of the second phase in August 1980, under which 260 branches were allocated to the various banks. At this time there were already 20 banks in operation as against 18 during the first phase. These branches were expected to start operation within 41 months but not later than December 1983.

While the first phase had 94 per cent performance ratio, the second phase had 68 per cent and many reasons have been suggested for this shortage of infrastructure in the rural areas; declining bank profitability especially in the period 1982-83; large number of branch allocations; lack of patronage of rural branches and a host of others. If the plan had gone through successfully, the country would have about 1,000 branches by the end of December 1983. The projection would have worked out to a simple average of 80,000 people to one branch of a bank–still a very low ratio by any standard.

By the end of December 1985, although two years behind, the second phase had achieved 93 per cent success with 248 completions out of 266 allocations.

In 1985, a 4-year third phase of the scheme was launched, lasting from August 1, 1985 to July 31, 1989. The third phase was aimed at establishing a further 300 rural bank branches with 28 commercial banks participating.

These rural branches were intended to further enhance the mobilisation of funds, help to promote the banking habit, create employment opportunities, facilitate the development of the financial system and encourage the rapid development of the rural areas. By the end of December 1985 there were 1,297 bank branches in Nigeria: 847 urban branches and 450 rural branches, as against 740 urban and rural branches by the end of December 1980.

SERVICE QUALITY IN BANKING

Almost every day new banks are emerging in the market, offering new products often cheaper in price. Intensifying competition has led many banks to seek new and more profitable ways to differentiate themselves. One strategy that has been related to success is the delivery of high service quality (Rudie and Wansley 1985).

A recent trend in many service industries is to consider service quality as a critical factor in gaining a competitive edge. Service quality enables organisations to achieve a differential advantage over their competitors. Several authors (including, Buzell and Wiersema 1981; Garvin 1983) argue that quality has a direct bearing on an organisation's performance and future growth. Furthermore, Buzzell and Wiersema (1981) established a positive link between quality and return on investment. However, according to Le Blanc and Nguyen (1988) the direct and indirect costs of mediocre quality in service industries can reach proportions of up to 40% of revenues.

Quality is meeting or exceeding customer's requirements and expectations (Creedon 1988). Quality is the ability to give your customers what they want and is based upon the customer's actual experience with the product or service. However, giving the customer what he wants might not be enough to retain him for very long. Ansell (1993) concluded that, the customer should also get a little bit extra. This extra is the 'glue' that binds the customers to the company, building long-term loyalty. Although much has been written on quality over the last decade, there still is no universal agreement on exactly what quality means. Crosby (1979) has defined quality as, "the compliance to specifications." Other definitions are similar, almost all of them revolving around providing what the customer wants (Stafford 1994).

Many definitions view service quality as, the degree of discrepancy between consumer's perceptions and expectations. Lewis and Booms (1983) define delivering quality service as, conforming to customer expectations on a consistent basis. Others (e.g., Parasuraman 1988, Avkiran 1994) add perceived service quality is a global judgement on attitude, related to superiority of the services, whereas satisfaction is related to a special transaction.

In terms of banking, quality is based on the service the bank provides its customers and is a complex whole encompassing such things as the customer interface activities, the rate of return on investment and other elements. Some of these elements of service quality have traditionally been regarded as marketing activities such as, the product and place (which includes location, opening times, facilities, etc.).

MEASURING SERVICE QUALITY

Any successful quality programme depends on having appropriate measurement techniques. Evans and Lindsay (1996) argue that measuring customer satisfaction and the service quality gap allows a business to discover customer perceptions and areas for improvements along with tracking trends to determine if changes result in improvements.

The primary consensus emerging from the service quality literature is that measuring service quality is problematic due to the unique characteristics of services (Zeithamal and Bitner 1996). The difficulties in the measurement of service quality gap is attributable to the fact that services are Intangible, Inseparable, Heterogenous and Perishable (Lovelock 1996; Zeithamal and Bitner 1996). Cowell (1991) also added Ownership. These characteristics also make it difficult for customers to evaluate services at the pre-consumption, consumption and post-consumption stages of the consumer decision making (Legg and Baker 1996) (these stages will be elaborated in the buying process discussed later). Organisations find it difficult to understand how customers are evaluating the quality of its services due to these unique characteristics (Zeithamal 1981).

The quality of service is not a uni-dimensional construct (Naser et al. 1999). Rather, it has been categorised in various dimensions relating to both core or process aspects of the service (Bitranand Lojo 1993; Gronroos 1984; Lewis 1993). Demings (1986) provides some important dimensions of service quality, these are: Time, Timeline, Completeness, Courtesy, Ethical, Accessibility, Accuracy, Responsiveness. Parasuraman, Zeithaml and Berry (1988) reduced the determinants of service quality to five dimensions as follows:

- *Tangibles:* Contains, physical facilities, equipment, and appearance of personnel.
- *Reliability:* Ability to perform the promised service dependably and accurately.
- *Responsiveness:* Willingness to help customers and provide prompt service.
- *Assurance:* Knowledge and courtesy of employees and their ability to inspire trust and confidence.
- *Empathy:* Caring, individualised attention the firm provides its customer.

THE BUYING PROCESS

People have various reasons for choosing a product, service or provider and many influences shape those reasons. Each of these major factors can in turn be divided into subgroups and the subject of research projects in their own right. The purpose here is to recognise that these influences exist, as some have been included in the questionnaire.

There are a number of models describing consumer buying behaviour, however, "there is a noticeable absence of any general conceptual framework that describes how consumers buy services in general, let alone financial services in particular" (McKechnie 1997). Some of the consumer models describing the purchase of goods go into great depth expanding the complete process such as those suggested by Sheth and Howard (1969), Engle et al. (1986), and Assael (1992). Other simple, more general models have also been suggested. At the heart of all these models (with slightly different terminology) are the basic five stages, suggested by Lancaster and Massingham (1993): Motivation, Search, Evaluation, Purchase, and Purchase Outcomes. The major influences on buying behaviour can be grouped into, Cultural, Social, Personal and Psychological factors (Kotler 1997).

There are many reasons why people are motivated to use a bank. Cowell (1991) said, "Needs and motives for the purchase of goods and services are much the same . . . However, one need that is important–in both situations–is the desire for personal attention." Good practitioners recognise the importance of personal attention in the sales situation and this can often be seen to represent 'the quality of service' provided by a business. Although developed for an industrial buying situation the IMP group (Hakansson 1982) showed the importance of the interaction between buyer and seller and a study by Paliwoda and Druce (1988) suggested that 'bonds' develop between buyer and seller. This view is shared by McKechnie (1997) when she concludes that, "Rather than develop a specific set of ideas and approaches for financial services, it would appear that the framework adopted by the interaction approach already has potential for general application in services as well as financial services."

The specific criteria used by each individual in evaluating a bank would be impractical to determine, therefore for the research a list of criteria based on the factors discussed in the service quality literature has been developed. Similar factors to those stated in service quality have been used by Arora et al. (1985) in their study on 'choice criteria used in financial institutions,' and strengthen the justification for their use in this study.

RESEARCH METHODS

Quality is one of the most effective and important factors which affect customers' perceptions towards the banks' image. High service quality can attract customers, while poor service quality can discourage them. Banks should concentrate their efforts on providing good service quality and satisfy their customers. Satisfied customers are most likely to continue purchasing banks' products and services and reflect strong loyalty towards their bank. Customer satisfaction is related to certain aspects of service quality such as convenience, competitiveness and location of service provider.

Banks should have a system in place to understand their customer's requirement, needs and wants. Management needs to have a good quality policy, which will strengthen the competitiveness of the bank.

The initial part of the study examines the factors that influence a firm's selection of a particular bank. The second part identifies firm's perceptions of a bank's service quality. The questionnaire was designed to gather information with regard to factors that influence the selection process and also to allow respondents to comment about the qualitative relationship between them and their respective banks.

QUESTIONNAIRE

The questionnaire study was structured to illustrate the possible character and quality of financial relations between banks and small and medium size firms. The sample included 150 small medium size firms.

The questionnaires for the firms were sent to either the Chairman or the management members of the firm, together with a covering letter explaining the importance of the project under research and the vital role played by each respondent in the successful completion of this project. After two weeks, thirty out of one hundred and fifty questionnaires were returned. Over a month had been allowed for the return of the questionnaires because of the wide geographical distribution of the Nigerian firms canvassed. Thereafter, a second set of questionnaires were sent out together with a covering letter, and followed by a third reminder letter emphasising the importance of the respondent's contribution to the study. These covering letters and subsequent telephone call gave a good response rate.

SAMPLE GROUPS

Sole trader companies had the majority 40%, Government sectors and limited liability companies were made up to 50% of the whole analysed group. Other status constitute 10%, as shown in Table 1.

TABLE 1. Status of Group

Status	Number of Firms	%
Sole proprietorship	60	40%
Civil Corporation	30	20%
Limited Liability Company	45	30%
Others	14	10%

Most of the companies in the sample were established after 1980. Only 20% started operations before that time. The number of new companies in years following 1980 spreads quite evenly.

Table 2 shows the firms' ownership structure. The majority of firms are private, domestic-owned companies (66.6%).

RESEARCH FINDINGS AND ANALYSIS: WHY FIRMS CHOOSE A PARTICULAR BANK

In the beginning of the nineties, small businesses had no options but to seek the service provided by banks. This situation changed subsequently and the number of banks offering services to small and medium business increased significantly. In 1990, there were 120 commercial banks with branches providing services all over Nigeria. But there was no clear difference between products and services offered by different banks.

A question was asked among managers of 150 companies in Nigeria on which bank was best known to them, and their response is summarized in Table 3.

Banks mentioned more frequently are those institutions which have very long banking traditions.

As seen from Table 4, the main source of start-up finance for small and medium firms were their own savings (20%), bank loans (13.3%) and loans from friends and relatives.

According to the pecking order theory, "investment is financed first with internal funds, reinvested earnings primarily; then by new issues of debt; and finally with new issues of equity" (Brealey & Myers, 2000). Equity is a last resort when the company runs out of debt capacity. But in case of Nigerian firms equity is the first choice of finance as seen from the results of the survey (Table 4).

TABLE 2. Sample Group (Ownership Structure)

	Number of Firms	%
Domestic Private Owners	100	66.6%
Foreign Private Owners	10	6.6%
Domestic & Private Owners	27	18%
Domestic Public & Private Owners	8	5%
Joint Domestic & Foreign Public & Private Owners	5	3.3%

TABLE 3. List of Top Eight Banks

Name of Banks	%
First Bank of Nigeria Plc	25.5
Union Bank of Nigeria Plc	20
United Bank of Africa Plc	18
Guarantee Trust Bank	15
Afri-Bank Plc	15
Savannah Bank Plc	12
Citi Bank Plc	10.5
National Bank Plc	10

TABLE 4. Start-Up Source of Finances in Representative Group

Sources	Number of Firms	%
Own Savings	70	46.6%
Loan from Bank	30	20%
Loan from Friend & Relative	20	13.3%
Loan from Supplier	18	12%
Others	12	8%

Table 5 shows an illustration on the distance from the firm to bank in km.

As seen from Table 6, the key features in selecting a particular bank are obviously credibility, location and the range of services. Other factors such as service and settlements time, staff competence, quality of

TABLE 5. Distance from Firm to Bank

KM Status	Number of Firms	%
Less than 2	70	46.6%
3-7	40	26.6%
8-10	28	18.6%
More than 10	12	8%

TABLE 6. Reasons for Choosing the Banks

Reason	Number of Firms	%
Credibility	30	20
Suitable Location	29	19.3
Wide Range of Services	21	14
Service Time	18	12
Settlements Time	16	10.6
Staff Competence	15	10
Quality of Service	13	8.6
Loan Availability	8	5.3

service, loan availability, good interest and commission rates are also considered as part of this complex selection process.

LIST OF SERVICES PROVIDED BY BANKS TO SMALL MEDIUM BUSINESSES

The following services are offered by banks to small medium businesses:

- Settlement accounts
- Deposit
- Working capital loan
- Medium term loan
- Long term loan
- Foreign currency loan
- Additional service to deposit accounts
- Investment consulting

At present the scale of relations between banks and businesses in Nigeria, could be judged as very narrow often limited to a working capital loan. Most firms (65%) perceive the services related to bank loans are satisfactory, although are more demanding about other types of services as indicated in Table 7.

Although innovations in the sphere of banking products have been introduced quickly by all banks, companies in Nigeria only took advantage of banking invention to a limited extent. From the surveyed companies none of them utilises forfeiting and factoring. Only few use Internet banking (2.66%) and investment consulting (4%). Most companies use telephone banking (46.66%), leasing (33.3%) and payment card (13.33%) services as shown in Table 8.

Experience tends to suggest that in Africa, only the trader can visit banks daily to deposit their daily cash sales. It is clear that the cost to the bank of such a client would be high, since 40% of the clients are under this category.

TABLE 7. Relations Between Banks and Firms

	Yes	No
Is the company satisfied with the bank's loan offer?	65%	20%
Are the procedures related to contracting a loan very inconvenient?	55%	31%
Does the company take under consideration the possibility to contract a non-banking loan?	30%	60%

TABLE 8. Innovation that Firm Operates

Innovation	Number of Firms	%
Telephone banking	70	46.66
Leasing	50	33.3
Payment card (value card)	20	13.33
Investment consulting	6	4
Internet banking	4	2.66
Factoring	0	0
Forfeiting	0	0

Service improvement can play an important role in the relations between firms and banks, especially since the majority of firms contact their banks everyday (40%), 2-3 times a week (23.3%) as shown in Table 9. Most companies queue up in their bank for about 5 to 10 minutes (43.3%), 10 to 15 minutes (26.66%), up to 5 minutes (23.33%) and more than 15 minutes (6.66%), as shown in Table 10.

Reducing the waiting time by being efficient and introducing technology such as telephone and internet banking can save time and cost for firms hence improving the image and reputation of the banks.

Table 11 clearly showed that there was a great level of dissatisfaction with some aspects of bank service quality. Complicated procedures and forms, queues, lack of individual approach and new technologies being

TABLE 9. How Often Companies Contact Banks

Frequency	Number of Firms	%
Everyday	60	40
2-3 times a week	35	23.33
Once a week on average	30	20
2-3 times a month	12	8
Once a month on average	8	5.33
Less than once a month	5	3.33

TABLE 10. Waiting Time for Service in Banks by Firms

Frequency	Number of Firms	%
Up to 5 minutes	35	23.33
5 to 10 minutes	65	43.3
10 to 15 minutes	40	26.66
More than 15 minutes	10	6.66

TABLE 11. Reason for Banks and Small Businesses Not Co-Operating in Nigeria

Elements	Number of Firms
Complicated Procedures and Forms	100
Queues	80
Lack of Individual Approach	77
Lack of New Technologies	75
Distance between Bank and Firm	66

mentioned as the main factors for dissatisfaction by the respondents and hence damaging the co-operation between firms and banks.

CONCLUSION

The findings of this research suggest that the key factors in selecting a particular bank are credibility, location and range of services. Interestingly, these results are similar with the results in developed countries as indicated by similar studies in developed countries (Parasuraman et al. 1985, 1988).

The qualitative characteristics of the service are becoming increasingly important. The majority of respondents are dissatisfied with the quality of services provided by banks in Nigeria. The research has indicated that complicated procedures and forms, queuing time, lack of individual approach and absence of new technology are some of the factors which create dissatisfaction and lack of co-operation between firms and banks.

It is recommended that commercial banks should investigate the cause of lack of service quality to firms. It was suggested in the literature that perceived service quality is a result of customer care and that this was due in large part to employee care. But, one should not simply jump to the conclusion that Nigerian banks' employees need training to handle customers in a more appropriate manner. The commercial banks need to examine all the other factors that give the overall perception of service quality. There are many issues involved with employee care, e.g., motivation rewards, etc., in addition to the training element. It is suggested that these issues along with the other factors briefly examined in this research be further explored in future research.

The other interesting point which emerged from this study is that firms, being customers of the banks, can express their dissatisfaction and banks could be accountable to firms. The important question that needs to be addressed is "What type of regulatory structure and legal system are desirable in Africa to make banks accountable and to ensure that loans could not go to individuals as a result of political influence and corruption." A further study is suggested by looking at the type of firms and the type of banks and services in order to make some more concrete analysis that would be useful for making policy improvements in Africa in general and Nigeria in particular.

REFERENCES

Ansell, T. (1993), *"Managing for quality in the financial service industry"* Chapman and Hall.

Avkiran, N.K. (1994), "Developing an instrument to measure customer service quality in banking" International Journal of Bank Marketing, Vol. 12, No. 6. pp. 10-18.

Bitran, G. and Lojo, M. (1993), "A framework for analysing the quality of the customer interface," *European Management Journal*, Vol. 11, No. 4, December, pp. 385-96.

Beer, M., Spector B., Lawrence P., Mills D., and Walton R. (1985), *"Human Resource Management: A General Manager's Perspective."* The Free Press.

Blanchard, R.F., and Galloway, R.L. (1994), "Quality in retail banking" *International Journal of Service Industry Management*, Vol. 5, No. 4.

Brandi, J. (1999), *"Customer Care Bulletin,"* April Issue.

Chachi, A. (1989), *Islamic Banking, Ph.D. thesis,* University of Wales Bangor, UK.

Collard, R. (1992), *"Total Quality: The Role of Human Resources"* in Strategies for Human Resource Management, Kogan Page Limited, London, U.K.

Cronin, J.J. and Taylor, S.A. (1994), "Servperf Versus Servqual: Reconciling Performance-Based and Perceptions-Minus-Expectations Measurement of Service Quality," *Journal of Marketing*, Vol. 58, pp. 125-131.

Crosby, P.B. (1979), *Quality Is Free,* McGraw-Hill, New York, USA.

Demings, E.W. (1986), *"Out of the Crisis"* MIT Press, Cambridge, MA, USA.

Evans, J.R. and Lindsay, W.M. (1996), *"The management and control of quality "* 3rd Edition, Printed by West Publishing Company.

Garvin, D.A. (1983), "Quality on the line," *Harvard Business Review*, September-October.

Gronroos, C. (1982), "Strategic Management and Marketing in the Service Sector," Swedish School of Economics and Business Administration, Helsinki, Finland.

Gronroos, C. (1984), "A service quality model and its marketing implications," *European Journal of Marketing*, Vol. 18, pp. 35-44.

Guest, D.E. (1987), "Human resource management and industrial relations," *Journal of Management Studies*, 24(50: 503-21).

Kwan, W. & Hee, T.J. (1994), "Measuring Service Quality in Singapore Retail Banking A Gap Analysis and Segmentation Approach," *Singapore Management Review*, Vol. 16, Part 2, pp. 1-24.

LeBlanc, G. and Nguyen, N. (1988), "Customers' Perceptions of Service Quality in Financial Institutions," *International Journal of Bank Marketing*, Vol. 6, No. 4, pp. 7-18.

Legg, D. and Baker, J. (1996), "Advertising Strategies for Service Firms," in Lovelock, C.H., *Services Marketing*, 3rd ed., Prentice Hall, Englewood Cliffs, NJ.

Lehtinen, U. and Lehtinen, J.R. (1982), "The Incline of Quality," *Harvard Business Review*, Vol. 60, September/October, pp. 163-71.

Lewis, R.C. and Booms, B.H. (1983), "The Marketing Aspects of Service Quality," in Berry, L., Shostack, G.L. and Upah, G. (Eds). *Emerging Perspectives on Services Marketing*, American Marketing Association, Chicago, pp. 99-104.

Lewis, B.R. (1989), "Quality in the service sector: A Review" *International Journal of Bank Marketing* (No. 5), 4-12.

Lewis, B.R. (1993), "Service quality; recent developments in financial services," *International Journal of Bank Marketing*, Vol. 11, No. 6, pp. 19-25.

Lewis, B.R. and Entwistle, T.W. (1990), "Managing the service encounter: a Focus on the Employee," *International Journal of Service Industry Management*, Vol. 1, No. 3, pp. 41-52.

Lovelock, C. (1996), *Services Marketing*, 3rd ed., Prentice Hall, Englewood Cliffs, NJ.

Naser, K., Jamal, A., and Al-Khatib, K. (1999). "Islamic banking: a study of customer satisfaction and preferences in Jordan." *International Journal of Bank Marketing* 17/3, pp. 135-150.

Parasuraman, A., Zeithaml, V.A., and Berry, L.L. (1985), " A conceptual model of service quality and its implications for future research" *Journal of Marketing*, Vol. 49, Fall, pp. 41-50.

Parasuraman, A., Zeithaml, V.A. and Berry, L.L. (1988), "SERVQUAL: A multiple-item scale for measuring consumer perceptions of service quality" *Journal of Marketing*, Vol. 64, No. 1, Spring.

Rudie, M.J. and Wansley, H.B. (1985), "The Merrill Lynch Quality Program," in *Services Marketing in a Changing Environment*, Thomas Bloch, Gregory Upah and Valarie A. Zeithaml (eds), Chicago, IL; American Marketing Association.

Stafford, M.R. (1994), "How customers perceive service quality" *Journal of Retail Banking*, Vol. XVll, No. 2 Summer.

Soyode, A. and Oyejide, T.A. (1975), "Branch Network and Economic Performance: A Case Study of Nigeria's Commercial Banks" *Nigerian Journal of Economic and Social Studies*, Vol. 17, No. 2, pp. 119-133.

Wilson, R. (1983), *Banking and finance in the Arab middle east*, Macmillan publisher ltd.

Woldie, A. and Dogan, I. (1996), "Service Quality Gap Analysis in the Turkish Retail Banks," *Middle East Business Review*, Volume 2, Number 1, pp. 28-44.

Zeithaml, V.A. (1981), "How consumer evaluation processes differ between goods and services," in Donnelly, J. and George, W. (Eds), *Marketing of Services*, American Marketing, Chicago, IL, pp. 186-90.

Zeithaml, V.A. and Bitner, M.J. (1996), *Services Marketing*, international edition, McGraw Hill.

How Have the Emerging Stock Exchanges in Africa Responded to Market Reforms?

Rose W. Ngugi
Victor Murinde
Christopher J. Green

SUMMARY. In this paper, we focus on how the stock markets in Africa have responded to the reform process. We identify three main types of reforms implemented in these markets since the 1990s, namely revitalization of the regulatory framework, modernization of trading systems, and relaxation of restrictions on foreign investors. We invoke market microstructure theory to hypothesize the expected response of the markets in terms of efficiency and volatility to the three types of reforms. Econometric methods are applied to test the hypotheses on a sample of ten

Rose W. Ngugi is affiliated with the Department of Economics, University of Nairobi; she is also affiliated with the Birmingham Business School, The University of Birmingham. Victor Murinde is affiliated with the Birmingham Business School, The University of Birmingham. Christopher J. Green is affiliated with the Department of Economics, Loughborough University.

Useful comments were received from participants at the conference on "Business and Development Finance," held at the University of Manchester, 5-6 April 2001. We thank the Department for International Development (DFID) for funding the research under the "Finance and Development Research Programme," Contract No. RSCI06506. Rose Ngugi also thanks Africa Economic Research Consortium (AERC) for the financial support in pursuit of her PhD programme. This paper is curved from Rose Ngugi's PhD thesis. The interpretations and conclusions expressed in this paper are entirely those of the authors and should not be attributed in any manner to DFID or AERC.

[Haworth co-indexing entry note]: "How Have the Emerging Stock Exchanges in Africa Responded to Market Reforms?" Ngugi, Rose W., Victor Murinde, and Christopher J. Green. Co-published simultaneously in *Journal of African Business* (International Business Press, an imprint of The Haworth Press, Inc.) Vol. 4, No. 2, 2003, pp. 89-127; and: *African Business Finance and Development Policy* (eds: Victor Murinde and Atsede Woldie) International Business Press, an imprint of The Haworth Press, Inc., 2003, pp. 89-127. Single or multiple copies of this article are available for a fee from The Haworth Document Delivery Service [1-800-HAWORTH, 9:00 a.m. - 5:00 p.m. (EST). E-mail address: docdelivery@haworthpress.com].

http://www.haworthpress.com/store/product.asp?sku=J156
10.1300/J156v04n02_06

stock exchanges, for the period 1988:01-1999:12. The evidence generally suggests that there are benefits of investments to improve market microstructure. For example, a comparative analysis across the sample demonstrates that markets with advanced trading technology, tight regulatory system and relaxed foreign investors' participation show greater efficiency and lower market volatility. Although direction of causality between efficiency and volatility varies across the markets, in general, we infer that reforms, which reduce volatility, reap higher efficiency. However, in some markets, the effects of the reforms are too recent to show any clear response pattern. *[Article copies available for a fee from The Haworth Document Delivery Service: 1-800-HAWORTH. E-mail address: <docdelivery@haworthpress.com> Website: <http://www.HaworthPress.com> © 2003 by The Haworth Press, Inc. All rights reserved.]*

KEYWORDS. Emerging stock markets, Africa, market reform

INTRODUCTION

Most African countries are revitalising existing stock markets and establishing new ones in order to facilitate the mobilisation of long-term finance. The revitalisation process has involved considerable investment to improve the market microstructure, including the shift from a manual to an automated trading system and the strengthening of the legal and regulatory framework. The improvements in market microstructure are expected to enhance market efficiency, facilitate increased liquidity, reduce trading costs as well as information asymmetry, and strengthen investors' confidence.

It may be argued that for the emerging stock markets in Africa, the drive to achieve market efficiency is desirable if stock markets are to play a vital role in the development process. Efficiency allows agents to diversify their sources of investment capital and spread investment risk by aggregating and conveying information through price signals (Amihud et al., 1990; Caprio and Demirgüç-Kunt, 1998). In addition, efficient stock prices and yields provide benchmarks against which the cost of capital for and returns on investment projects can be judged, even if such projects are not, in fact, financed through the stock market (Green, Maggioni and Murinde, 2000). In addition, as the stock prices are forward looking, they provide a unique record of the shifts in investors' views about the future prospects of companies as well as the economy. Further, an efficient price discovery process is traditionally associated with low volatility, which promotes stock market effectiveness in allocating resources efficiently. High volatility distorts efficient resource allocation by making investors more averse to hold stocks. Risk-averse investors tend to demand a high-risk premium, which increases the cost of capital and reduces the level of investment (see Bekaert and Harvey, 1997; Kim and Singal, 2000). Market liquidity is desirable because it reduces the required return by investors; illiquidity increases the cost of capital and acts as a constraint for stock markets to adequately perform their information processing and signalling functions (Amihud et al., 1997). Thus, if it has an efficient price discovery process, no excess volatility, and provides liquidity at low cost, the stock market can make important contributions to the development process.

The important question, therefore, is whether by undertaking the revitalisation process, emerging markets in Africa have attained positive value, in terms of efficiency, liquidity and volatility. Existing studies from emerging markets elsewhere report mixed results,[1] while studies on the emerging stock market in Africa were carried out before the reform period, and therefore, tell us very little about the response of the markets to the reform process.[2] The studies do not compare the period *before* and *after* the reforms or consider comparative analysis across the markets to see if there are any lessons to be learned from the markets that have advanced with the reforms.

This paper analyses the microstructure characteristics of emerging stock markets in Africa by comparing the markets not only before and after the reform period, but also across markets at different stages of the reform process. The idea is to assess the impact of the revitalisation process on the market microstructure characteristics of these markets. The integral elements of the revitalisation process of the markets are identified; these comprise the establishment of the market regulator, change in trading system, entry of foreign investors and expansion of brokerage firms.

The main contributions of the paper are two-fold. First, the paper innovatively implements a battery of econometric tests to study the main microstructure aspects of the emerging stock markets in Africa. Second, the paper generates evidence to compare the position *before* and *after* the reforms of the revitalisation process in terms of the identified main microstructure characteristics of the markets (efficiency and volatility).[3] One difficulty in undertaking the microstructure study of emerging stock markets in Africa is that most of the available data are of relatively recent origin, and some data are not easily available. In this context, the main shortcoming of this study is that due to lack of bid-ask data, the analysis on price discovery may be incomplete.

In what follows, the paper is structured into five sections. Section 2 examines the evolution and development of stock markets in Africa, focusing on the main institutional reforms. Section 3 sets out the theoretical framework for empirical analysis, while the data and econometric methodology are detailed in Section 4. Section 5 contains the empirical results. Section 6 concludes.

THE EVOLUTION OF EMERGING STOCK MARKETS IN AFRICA AND SUBSEQUENT POLICY REFORMS

There are 20 stock exchanges[4] in 19 African countries, one of which is a regional market (BRVM)[5] for eight countries. Strictly, some of the markets are classified by the IFC as emerging stock markets, for example, the Nigeria Stock Exchange (NISE) and Zimbabwe Stock Exchange (ZSE), while others are classified as frontier markets.

The development of stock markets in Africa tends to show an evolutionary process with various stages characterized by type of regulatory system, trading method and the scope for market participation. Ngugi (2001) discusses in detail the historical development of each of the African stock markets. In general, the markets started with no formally laid-down rules and regulations; trading activities were based on interpersonal relationships. Formal markets were then established, driven either by the desire of traders to diversify sources of investment funds or by the need of governments to establish a formal market to float their debt stocks. Formalization and revitalization process saw changes in the regulatory framework, trading system and composition of market investors.

Reforms in Stock Market Regulation

Most stock markets in Africa established or empowered existing market regulators during the revitalization process (e.g., NSE and ESE). The regulators were charged with the responsibility of promoting and facilitating the development of an orderly and efficient capital market. To achieve this objective, market authorities targeted to maintain surveillance over the security market, ensure fair and equitable dealings, undertake the licensing of members and protect investors against abuse of insider traders. Self-regulated markets saw amendments of the existing Stock Exchange Act to facilitate restructuring of the Exchange (e.g., JSE).

At the initial stages of the establishment of a legal entity some stock exchanges borrowed rules and regulations from established stock markets, which enhanced their credibility. Self-regulatory rules were introduced in the context of Rules and Regulation of Stock Exchange. For example, stockbrokers in the NSE borrowed rules and regulations from the London Stock Exchange (LSE) to facilitate the establishment of a legal entity. The LSE recognized the NSE as an independent overseas stock exchange and the exchange was finally established in 1954, adopting the 'Rules and Regulations of NSE 1954' that embodied the self-regulatory rules. Botswana Stock Exchange (BSE) initially operated under a set of interim regulation 1989-1995, which was applied with assistance from the Zimbabwe Stock Exchange (ZSE). The market gained a legal status in November 1995. JSE initially adopted rules and regulations for the conduct of share dealing and listing of companies, deciding on commission fees and selling members from Transvaal Share and Claim Exchange in Barberton. New rules and regulations were adopted later following those of the LSE amended to suit local circumstances. For GSE, the established Exchange in October 1990 was given recognition as an authorized stock exchange under the Stock Exchange Act of 1971 (Act 384).

As a first step toward government involvement in the operation of the market, some markets in Africa set up Capital Issue Committees (CIC) to monitor issues in the primary markets, for example, NSE and NISE. Market regulators were then established to act as conduits through which the government would monitor the activities of the stock market. For example, in NSE following the recommendations of IFC/CBK study report, the government set up a Capital Market Development Advisory Council whose role was to work out modalities necessary to establish Capital Market Authority (CMA) in November 1988. CMA was constituted in January 1990 after the Bill (Capital Market Authority Act cap 485 A) was passed by Parliament in November 1989. For the NISE, a market regulator was established before the mounting of reform program. The SEC Degree No. 71 established a regulator in 1979, abolishing the CIC. In GSE, Security Industrial Law 1993 recognized the Security and Securities Commission as the apex regulatory body for securities in the stock market. ESE enacted a new Law (Law 95/1992)[6] in June 1992, which provided CMA established in 1980 with legal authority and status necessary to implement and enforce the needed legislation and regulation in the securities markets. The CMA then issued executive regulation in April 1993 and the Law came into force in 1994.

JSE is a self-regulatory organization governed by a set of rules drawn up by the JSE Committee. The Registrar of Stock Exchanges approves JSE rules, which must comply with the requirement set out in Stock Exchange Control Act (SECA). SECA of 1947 gave the JSE self-regulatory rules forces of law that were not enjoyed previously; the Act was amended in 1985. In the reform process, the Act was amended spelling out a new structure for JSE. In 1992, JSE Committee formed a research sub-Committee to research an appropriate future structure for JSE. The sub-Committee presented a 500-page report to the Committee in 1994 and the proposed amendments were approved by Parliament in September 1995. The proposed restructuring impacted on membership, trading principle and systems, clearing and settlement, transfer and registration, capital requirements of member firms and the financial structure of the JSE. The proposed reforms were aimed at improving the liquidity of the JSE.

Reforms in the Trading System

Initially, in most stock markets in Africa, trading was carried out by phone; in most cases, stockbrokers met to exchange prices over a cup of coffee. Trading was based on a gentleman's agreement where standard commissions were charged while clients were obliged to honor their contractual commitment of making good delivery and settling relevant costs of trading. Gradually, or in some cases as part of the reform process, trading forums shifted from coffeehouses to the trading floor and screen trading. For example, NSE shifted to floor trading in 1991, phasing out the coffeehouse forum. Some markets have gradually expanded the number of trading floors; for example, NISE had six trading floors by 1990 having opened Kaduna (in 1978), Port Hartcourt (in 1980), Kano (in 1989), Onista (in 1990) and Ibadan (in 1990).

Only a few markets in Africa have adopted the modern trading technology, gradually phasing out the manual trading cycle. The main objective of the reform has been to reduce the transaction period and increase market liquidity. JSE gradually phased out open outcry trading floor for three months starting March 1996 and finally closed the floor in 7th June 1996, replacing it with fully automated electronic trade in respect of all listed securities on JSE Equities Trading (JET) system.[7] ESE introduced a computerized trading system in February 1995 allowing automatic matching between buyers and sellers; this also allowed the increase in trading hours by 50%. NISE introduced the computerized central security clearing settlement depository and custodian system in April 1997. In January 1997, MSE established electronic clearing and settlement system, which facilitated the shift from three days trading to five days or daily trading in November 1997. In 1998, the Central Depository System was implemented, allowing delivery versus payment on a T + 5 day rotating basis. NSE is in the initial stages of introducing electronic central depository system. GSE commenced a manual centralized clearing and settlement system on 26 April 1996. The system operates within a set of rules approved by GSE Council and the SEC and it has allowed the minimization of trade failure and strengthened the level of coordination between brokers and the registrar.

In general, however, trading days and duration vary across the markets in Africa. The average trading period is two hours a day while the transaction period ranges from T + 7 to T + 3. Stockbrokers acting as agents, rather than principals, dominate trading activity. Only JSE allow stock-broking firms the choice of dealing in single or dual capacity, following the Stock Exchange Amendment Act, 1995. With dual capacity, a member acts as either an agent on behalf of or deals as a principal with a client. Stockbrokerage is fully negotiable with clients unlike markets where the Stock Exchange spells out the brokerage commission for clients as a regressive rate to the amount traded.

In some markets, the stockbrokerage activities are restricted to local firms, while in other markets, the size of the stockbrokerage industry is restricted. For example, while initially stockbrokerage in the JSE was limited to South African citizens, in November 1995, the Stock Exchange Control Act opened stockbrokerage membership to non-citizens and foreign corporate entries. For the NSE, the number of stockbrokers remained constant at six till 1994, when new brokers were licensed. The range of assets traded is very narrow; only on the JSE and the NASE are derivatives traded. The majorities of the markets deal in shares, government bonds and corporate bonds.

Relaxation of Restrictions on the Participation of Foreign Investors

There are variations on the level of participation of foreign investors in the stock markets in Africa. The opening of portfolio investment to foreign investors was part of the reform process, which saw relaxation of capital controls. Stock markets established during the colonial days saw a period of foreign domination during the initial stages, but after political independence, efforts were made to encourage the participation of local investors and to restrict the participation of foreign investors. Later, during the reform process, regulations were relaxed to allow unrestricted participation by foreign investors.

Initially, in 1972, the Nigerian Enterprise promotion Decree obliged some foreign companies to sell part of their holdings to domestic investors. Foreign companies operating in Nigeria were expected to extend equity participation to the wider public. The 1977 indigenisation program required some categories of enterprises to either be left entirely or partially (60%) to Nigerians. However, the 1989 Nigerian enterprise promotion Decree No. 54 amended the Indigenisation Decree allowing foreign investors 100% participation in some securities, while 40% holding ceiling was retained for banking and insurance, petroleum prospecting and mining industries. The Nigerian Investment Promotion Commission Decree No. 16 of 1995 allowed up to 100% foreign ownership of any Nigerian company. A legislation-captioned foreign exchange (monitoring and miscellaneous provision) No. 17 Jan 16 1995 further eased the mechanism for foreign investment flows by providing easy movement of capital especially the foreign portfolio investors. This repealed the exchange control of 1962 allowing establishment of autonomous foreign exchange market, free transactions in foreign exchange at market rate and permitted unrestricted import and export of foreign exchange. Those in second tier market were 100% locally owned. For NSE market, the government adopted indigenisation policy after independence in 1963, to allow the local citizens to take control of economic activities while at the same time the government protected the interests of the foreign investors by passing the Foreign Investment Protection Act (1964). Capital controls were relaxed in 1995 and this allowed the foreigners up to 20% of the equity for inward portfolio investment, and then revised to 40% in June 1995. In the ZSE, a set of investment guidelines was announced in April 1993 to encourage the inflow of foreign portfolio investors. Currently, there are no prior exchange control approvals necessary for foreign investors' participation in ZSE. However, inward transfer of foreign currency through normal banking channels finances foreign investors. The participation of foreign investors has now increased to 40% and 10% respectively. In case where foreign investors exceed the 10% limit, the investor is directed to sell the excess shares within 60 days. There is 100% after tax remittance; free remittance of capital and capital gain subject to control approval for importation of capital; and freedom to register shares in their name or names of nominees companies. Foreign investors may also bring in hard currency to invest up to a maximum of 15% of their assets in primary issues of bonds and stocks. The MSE opened to foreign investors in 1994 with the abolition of exchange controls and the Stock Exchange (Investment by foreign investors) Rules 1994. Foreigners subscribe to new issues of shares of company listed in stock exchange and also invest in unit trust. Foreign investors do not need approval to trade shares unless the investment is for the purpose of legal or management control of a Mauritius company. The only restriction is that the foreign investors cannot have individual holdings of more than 15% in a Sugar Company. In the BSE, foreign investors are not allowed to own more than 10% of issued capital of a publicly quoted company and foreign ownership of the free stock of a local company trading on the exchange not to exceed 55%. There are restrictions on the repatriation of funds where amounts up to P100m can be repatriated immediately, and amount exceeding this requires to be repatriated over a specified period. Ghana Investment Promotion Center Act 478 1994 allows free investment by non-residents through stock exchange without prior approval by government. However, there are restrictions where a maximum of 10% equity is allowed in a single quoted company for non-residents portfolio investor. For a single equity, foreign investors may hold up to a cumulative total of 74%. These limits exclude trade in Ashanti Goldfields shares. There is full and free foreign exchange remittance of initial capital, capital gains and other forms of earnings. The newly-created Tanzanian Stock Exchange does not allow foreigners to operate in the market. In the TSE, the foreigner can buy up to 10% of listed company and 30% of unlisted companies. In August 1995, the stock exchange issued a decree simplifying the purchase of shares by foreign investors.

Overall Reforms

Overall, therefore, we find that while the basic trading system is call over (order driven) some markets have shifted from floor trading to screen trading and others are phasing out the manual clearing and settlement system with electronic systems, while others have established central scrip depository. In other markets, doors have been opened for foreigners' participation in the brokerage activities, which were previously dominated by local participants. In addition, efforts have been made to reduce transaction costs including taxation of share trading earnings where for example, capital gain tax has been suspended and withholding taxes made final.[8] Relaxation of capital controls and participation of foreign investors in portfolio investment vary across the markets.

THE THEORY

We invoke market microstructure theory in order to provide a tractable framework for studying the response of the emerging stock markets in Africa to the reform process. The theory is particularly helpful in tracing the link between the institutional structure of a stock market and the main characteristics of the market, namely volatility, efficiency, cost of trading and liquidity. For example, comparing the developed stock markets and the developing stock markets, Demirgüç-Kunt and Levine (1996) and Kumar and Tsetsekos (1999) attribute the problems of information asymmetry, thin trading and shallow depth of emerging stock markets to weak institutional infrastructure. Moreover, Demirgüç-Kunt and Levine (1996) observe that stock markets with strong information disclosure laws, internationally accepted accounting standards and unrestricted international capital flows tend to have larger and more liquid markets; see also Khambata (2000).

Based on the existing literature, we hypothesize the theoretically expected response of the microstructure characteristics of emerging stock markets in Africa (i.e., market efficiency, volatility and liquidity) to the three main institutional reforms that have underpinned the reform process in these markets, namely changes in the trading system, establishment of market regulator, and entry of foreign investors.

First, in theory, the shift in the trading system from a call to an open outcry floor trading is expected to increase market liquidity and enhance transparency, thus reducing microstructure costs and volatility (Pagano and Röell, 1996).[9] The literature also shows the call auction market to be more efficient than the continuous auction markets; the former is also shown to enhance liquidity and reduce market volatility (Madhavan, 1992).[10] This is because the call auction imposes an effective mechanism for dealing with asymmetric information problems, where the imposed delays in execution of trades forces traders to reveal information through their order placements (Comerton-Forde, 1999).

Second, with respect to the entry of the market regulator, the theory stipulates that this should signal strengthening of the legal and regulatory frameworks, which act to promote market efficiency by providing transparency, immediacy and equal access in the disclosure of information. Information symmetry also reduces market volatility. This also increases liquidity by enhancing investors' confidence to commit their resources to the stock market (see Röell, 1992; Demirgüç-Kunt and Levine, 1996; Khambata, 2000).

Third, the entry of foreign investors in emerging markets is theoretically expected to enhance stock price stability, increase liquidity of the market, promote efficiency and lengthen investor's horizon (Aitken, 1998; Richards, 1996). However, if the market is thin, and has low quality and small capitalisation shares, this would reduce the market capacity to absorb foreign capital inflows and would thus subject the market to excess volatility or cause overheating in the domestic economy. In addition, opening the market exposes it to foreign factors such that volatility in foreign prices may cause domestic prices to be volatile (Kim and Singal, 2000). Consequently, shareholders ask for higher risk premium, thus increasing the cost of capital and reducing investment.

Table 1 summarizes the above theoretically expected responses of the revitalization reforms on microstructure characteristics of the emerging stock markets in Africa. Almost all the hypothesized effects are unambiguous, except the effect of the entry of foreign investors on volatility, which may be positive or negative depending on market size.

DATA AND ECONOMETRIC METHODOLOGY

Sample Selection and Data

Our main source of data was the annual series of the IFC Emerging Markets Fact Book for the period 1989-2000. We collected data for local market indices and other series at local currencies. The Consumer Price Index data were collected from International Financial Statistics and then harmonized to the base year 1995. JSE index data was only available from 1994, we extended the series backward using data from

TABLE 1. The Theoretically Expected Response of Revitalisation Reforms on Microstructure Characteristics

	Efficiency	Volatility	Liquidity*
1. Changes in trading system			
1.1 Call to open outcry floor trading	+	-	+
1.2 Call auction to continuous auction	+	-	+
2. Establishment of market regulator	+	-	+
3. Entry of foreign investors	+	±	+

Note: * we do not empirically study liquidity in this paper because of data inconsistency across the markets in Africa

the JSE research division. Similarly GSE series was extended backward using data from CEPA, Ghana.

Out of the total population of 19 emerging stock markets in Africa, we used the criterion of data availability to select a sample of ten stock exchanges for analysis, namely the JSE, NISE, ZSE, NSE, MSE, CSE, ESE, TSE, BSE and GSE. The sample however is characterized by non-uniform time series across the markets. For example, JSE index is available for the period 1980:01-1999:12, NISE, NSE and ZSE for 1988:01-1999:12 only while GSE was available for the period 1990:11-1999:12 and MSE 1991:06-1999:12. The rest of the sampled markets had data available for the period 1996:01-1999:12. Consequently, we analyzed the period 1988:01-1999:12. It was not possible to capture impact of some reforms, for example, we cannot analyze the entry of foreign investors in August 1995 for TSE, and the introduction of electronic trading on the CSE in 1993.

Table 2 reports the descriptive statistics for the sample markets covering the period 1990:01-1999:12. The skewness statistics indicates that most of the markets have upper thicker tails than the lower tails, while the kurtosis indicates most of the markets except for ZSE and CSE have thicker tails than the normal distribution. Thus, we conclude that stock market returns are non-normally distributed.

Estimation and Testing Procedures

In the light of the overview of the emerging stock markets in Africa (Section 2) and the theory predicting the market microstructure response to institutional reforms (Section 3), we aim to model the main

TABLE 2. Descriptive Statistics for Stock Returns for the Surveyed Markets

Market	Mean	Median	Maximum	Minimum	Std deviation	Skewness	Kurtosis
JSE	.0088	.0161	.1614	−.3548	.0615	−1.7178	11.9407
MSE	.100	.0054	.1552	−.1148	.0470	.3975	4.0673
NISE	.0232	.0198	.2139	−.1858	.0506	.3149	7.6573
NSE	.0086	.0006	.4181	−.2071	.0759	1.8662	11.1797
ZSE	.0234	.0370	.2309	−.2276	.0904	−.3464	3.111
GSE	.0207	.0028	.4431	−.1413	.0832	2.1944	10.7238
ESE	.0194	.0078	.2681	−.0602	.0525	1.8259	7.9294
CSE	.0192	.0131	.1484	−.1193	.0534	.1189	3.116
TSE	.0053	.006	.1694	−.1632	.0495	.3763	6.9510
BSE	.0305	.0130	.2688	−.0513	.0630	1.7409	6.3218

market microstructure characteristics of the markets, namely market efficiency and volatility, during the reform process. Below, we consider each one in turn.

Testing for Market Efficiency

To explore market efficiency for each of the sample stock exchanges, we start by testing for weak form efficiency. In the context of the Efficient Market Hypothesis (EMH), stock prices are modeled as a random walk process (Fama, 1970); thus, we infer weak form efficiency when the stock price is integrated of order one. If we define stock returns as the first difference of logged stock prices then weak form efficiency is inferred when stock returns are I(0). We use the Augmented Dickey-Fuller (ADF) and the Phillips-Perron (PP) unit root tests to analyze the random walk component in the series. The lag length is selected using the AIC and SC criteria. We also use the serial correlation test for weak form efficiency; this tests the assumption that with a random walk process the error term is identically and independently distributed.[11] We test for first order serial correlation using an autoregressive process, as follows:

$$R_t = \alpha + \mu_t \tag{1}$$

$$\mu_t = \rho\mu_t + \varepsilon_t \tag{2}$$

where μ_t is the unconditional residual compiled by applying the regression coefficient to the independent variables; μ_{t-1} is the information from the previous period; and ε_t is the innovation in disturbance.[12] Substituting (2) into (1), we obtain:

$$R_t = \beta + \rho R_{t-1} + \varepsilon_t \tag{3}$$

where $\beta = \alpha(1-\rho)$. We thus test the hypothesis that RHO $(\rho) = 0$, i.e., no serial correlation. Weak form efficiency is inferred when $\rho = 0$, thus we can define this point as the efficiency frontier. Therefore, any dispersion from this point implies deviation from market efficiency where the larger the absolute value of dispersion (as indicated by the magnitude of ρ), the farther away is the market from achieving efficiency. The sign value of ρ reflects on the period when predictability is implied. Positive value implies predictability in the short run, while negative value implies predictability in the long run. If market reforms are aimed at enhancing the performance of the market, then we expect that in the post reform period markets are more efficient and therefore the value of ρ is lower than in the 'before' period. In addition, comparing markets at different stages of institutional development we expect markets that have adequately implemented market reforms will reflect more market efficiency. Therefore a market with weak institutional set up will show more dispersion from the efficiency frontier and a higher absolute value of ρ.

Further we test for mean reversion following the argument by Fama and French (1988) and Summers (1986) that predictability of returns is attributable to a slowly decaying stationary component of stock prices. Unit root tests do not distinguish between a stationary series and a series that is stationary but with a random walk component (Cochrane, 1988). Fama and French (1988) propose the use of long-horizon returns analysis to evaluate the importance of the mean reverting component of stock prices. This is a regression-based approach for mean reversion, which considers the pattern of autocorrelation function over increasing return horizons. We expect positive autocorrelation for short-term predictability and negative autocorrelation for long-term predictability of stock returns. Cochrane (1988) proposes the use of variance ratio of long differences to measure the size of random walk component in stock price series. This can be captured using the Blanchard and Quah (1989) VAR model, which isolates the temporary (non-stationary) and permanent (stationary) component in stock prices. The Blanchard-Quah technique imposes long-run restriction on the VAR to identify the permanent and temporary shocks in a multivariate time series context. We use the VAR model with the logarithm of stock prices and logarithm of consumer price index; this is a test for semi-strong efficiency, given that the inflation variable represents the argument that stock prices are predicted using public information.

Following Fama and French (1988), Summers (1986) and Majnoni and Mussa (2001) we assume the observed stock price (p_t) has two components: the efficient price (m_t) attributed to the expected value of the security on basis of public information; and a pricing error (s_t) measuring the duration of price observed in the market from:

$$p_t = m_t + s_t \qquad (4)$$

m_t is a random walk component with no serial correlation problem.

$$m_t = m_{t-1} + w_t \tag{5}$$

where $Ew_t = 0$; $Ew^2_t = \sigma^2_w$; $Ew_t w_s = 0$ for $t \neq s_t$ is expressed as a first order autoregressive process:

$$s_t = \alpha w_t + \eta_t \tag{6}$$

where w is the component correlated with arrival of information on the market and η is the innovation. Defining stock return as the log difference of stock prices then,

$$R_t = p_t - p_{t-1} = m_t + m_{t-1} + s_t - s_{t-1} = w_t + s_t - s_{t-1} \tag{7}$$

which can be expressed as a moving average of a white noise process assuming no correlation between w and s.

$$R_t = \varepsilon_t - \alpha\varepsilon_{t-1} \tag{8}$$

If we assume deviations are due to information shocks and not innovation shock ($\eta = 0$), we can express the information shock variance (σ^2_w) and pricing error variance (σ^2_s) as:

$$\sigma^2_w = (1-\alpha)^2\sigma^2_\varepsilon$$
$$\sigma^2_s = \alpha^2\sigma^2_\varepsilon \tag{9}$$

Thus, the total variance is defined by both the variance of the price error and random walk variances. The ratio of the price error variance to the random walk variance defines market efficiency; efficiency is attained when the ratio is zero, and the higher the ratio, the more inefficient is the market.[13]

We also apply the Blanchard and Quah (1989) to transform the vector autoregressive (VAR) model into a vector moving average (VMA) model. We start with a standard VAR model:

$$\beta X_{it} = \Gamma_0 + \Gamma_1 X_{t-1} + \varepsilon_{xit} \tag{10}$$

where X_{it} is a vector of the variables of interest. The innovations in this model are serially correlated, and thus, for estimation purposes we need a technical condition to ensure that the components can be uniquely represented as serially uncorrelated disturbances. By the multivariate form of Wold's decomposition, X has a moving average representation (Blanchard and Quah, 1989). We solve the problem by multiplying equation (10) with β^l to get the following:

$$X_{it} = \beta^{-1}\Gamma_0 + \beta^{-1}\Gamma_1 X_{it-1} + \beta^{-1}\varepsilon_{xit}$$

$$X_{it} = A_0 + A_1 X_{t-1} + e_t \tag{11}$$

where ε is the one step ahead forecast error in X_j; e is the error term; A_0 is contemporaneous effects and A_1 is the subsequent lag effects. Taking the first difference of the model we can then express X as a moving average function as follows:

$$X_t = A_0 e_t + A_1 e_{t-1} + \ldots\ldots$$

$$= \sum_{i=0}^{a} A_j e_{t-j} \tag{12}$$

where A_0 captures the contemporaneous effect of e on X and A_j is the subsequent lag effect. The differenced X is a stationary process; thus Blanchard and Quah (1989) assume neither of the shocks have long run effect on X_{is}, such that disturbances have a diagonal variance-covariance matrix. To express X_t in terms of the structural shocks, we can substitute for e_{it} which is expressed as $e_{it} = (1/\beta^{-1})\beta^{-1}\varepsilon_{it}$ to get:

$$X_t = \sum_{j=0}^{n} C_j v_{t-j} \tag{13}$$

To obtain the moving average we first estimate and then invert the vector autoregressive representation of X (Blanchard and Quah, 1989). The relationship between the vector of innovations and e the vector of original disturbance can be expressed as $v = A_0 e$ and $A_j = C_j A_0$ (which are the impulse responses) for all j. Thus, knowing A_0 allows one to recover e from v and A_j from C_j. Thus, to recover the temporary and permanent shocks from the VAR innovation, Blanchard and Quah (1989) suggest four restrictions, which can be obtained by normalising the variances to unity and requiring them to be orthogonal. Let Ω be the variance-covariance matrix of v_t, thus we can write the restrictions as

$A_0 A_0^{-1} = \Omega$. The fourth restriction on A_0 is expressed as $k^1 \sum_{j=0}^{\infty} C_j A_0 k = 0$

where $k = (1\ 0)^1$. We test for non-stationarity for the two variables and also test for cointegration to ensure they have a long-run relationship. There is no hypothetical relationship between the proportionate size of the stationary component, and the efficiency,[14] however finding the presence of stationary component, we conclude that stock returns are predictable.

Testing for Volatility

To investigate the impact of reforms on volatility, we analyse the second moments of the stock returns using a GARCH type model. We first observe the autocorrelation function and test for heteroscedasticity problem using the ARCH-LM test; where volatility clustering is indicated we use the GARCH-type model. Specifically, we use a generalised version due to Bollerslev (1986), the GARCH (p, q), which introduces long memory to the ARCH process via lagged conditional variance:

$$R_t = \mu_t + \varepsilon_t \tag{14}$$

$$\varepsilon_t / \Omega_{t-1} \approx N(0, h_t^2) \tag{15}$$

$$h_t^2 = w + \sum_{i=1}^{p} \alpha_i \varepsilon_{t-i}^2 + \sum_{j=1}^{q} \beta_j h_{t-j}^2 \tag{16}$$

$\varpi > 0;\ \alpha_1 \ldots \alpha_p \geq 0;\ \beta_1 \ldots \beta_q \geq 0$

where $R_{(t)}$ is continuously compounded return; $\mu_{(t)}$ = conditional mean; $\varepsilon(t)$ = residual; Ω_{t-1} = information available; h_t^2 = the conditional variance; α_i indicates the magnitude of the effect imposed by lagged error terms on conditional various, and thus tests for the existence of ARCH process in the error terms (or volatility clustering);[15] β_j are parameters that indicate the propensity of volatility shocks to persist over time. If the conditional variance is assumed to influence the mean returns *ex ante*, then Equation (17) becomes

$$R_t = \mu_t + \sigma h_t^2 + \varepsilon_t \tag{17}$$

defining a GARCH-M(p, q) model. σ is the risk preferencing parameter (time-varying premium); a positive value indicates that investors are risk averse and are being rewarded more for taking risk. A negative sign implies investors are risk lovers while a non-significant value implies the market does not price conditional variance.

To estimate the GARCH we need to specify an appropriate return-generating model, as misspecification of the mean equation would make the estimate of the variance inconsistent. We control for factors that contribute to statistical serial correlation such as thin trading. Given the various policy and institutional changes (Section 2), we test for the sensitivity of expected volatility to information held in past returns. This follows the argument that the sign of return variable influences future volatility where volatility is negatively correlated with the direction of actual price changes.[16]

When volatility clustering is absent, we measure volatility in terms of the squared standard deviations from recursive OLS estimation, following Green, Maggioni and Murinde (2000). To compare volatility across the markets we use descriptive statistics.

EMPIRICAL RESULTS

Test Results for Market Efficiency

Comparative Analysis of Efficiency Across the Markets

Table 3 reports the test results for market efficiency in the sampled markets. Part I of the table reports the unit root results using the ADF and PP tests. The results indicate stationary stock return series, which implies that stock returns are random walk processes and in the context of EMH, weak form efficiency is implied. These results are similar across the markets despite differences indicated in the institutional development of the markets. However, given that all the sample markets basically use periodic auction trading system, these results are consistent with the theoretical predictions that periodic price discovery processes have efficient prices (Madhavan, 1991).

The serial correlation test results are reported in Part II of Table 3. We run regression using the constant model where under the random walk hypothesis the constant should be insignificantly different from zero while the residual should be *IID* random variable. We test for the significance of first order serial correlation using *RHO (ρ)* to make conclu-

TABLE 3. Test Results for Market Efficiency

Part I reports the unit root results using the Augmented Dickey Fuller (ADF) and Philips and Perron (PP) tests for both stock return ($\Delta LOGINDEX$) and stock prices ($LOGINDEX$). Part II reports the first order serial correlation test results using Autoregressive (AR) process. We test the random walk hypotheses for zero mean and no serial correlation $p = 0$. The constant model is defined as $R_i = \alpha + \mu_i$. DW statistic for the AR model are calculated as $DW = 2\ (2'p)$. The critical value for ADF unit test at 10% is 2.5827 for all except CSE, TSE and BSE whose critical value is 2.6005 while for PP unit root test is 2.6013.

	ESE	JSE	GSE	MSE	NISE	NSE	ZSE	CSE	TSE	BSE
Part I Unit root results										
LOGINDEX										
ADF	.8444(2.5838)	-.7129	-.8193	-1.9690	-1.3218	-2.1010	-.2975	-1.7620	.0694	-.0730
AR(1)	.014	-.0211	-.0152	-.0380	-.0140	-.0624	-.0055	-.0488	.0034	-.0021
	(.8444)	(-.7129)	(-.8193)	(-1.9690)	(-1.3218)	(-2.1010)	(-.2975)	(-1.7620)	(.0694)	(-.0730)
PP	1.0672(2.5827)	-1.0258	-.9692	-1.9184	-1.2840	-2.0829	.5607	-1.7380	.1616	.1750
AR(1)	.0174	-.0274	-.0155	-.0370	-.0145	-.0641	.0168	-.0466	.0297	.0076
	(1.4398)	(-.9583)	(-.8466)	(-1.9142)	(-1.3107)	(-2.0795)	(.9574)	(-1.7626)	(.6625)	(.2738)
$\Delta LOGINDEX$										
ADF	-3.1662	-4.5429	-3.3965	-2.7990	-2.6241	-2.6593	-3.0113	-4.2818	-4.1847	-3.9061
	(2.5840)									
AR(1)	-.7354	-1.4290	-.6994	-.5635	-.4626	-.5743	-.4553	-.8475	-.7926	-.6639
	(3.1662)	(-4.5429)	(-3.3965)	(-2.7990)	(-2.6241)	(-2.6593)	(-3.0113)	(-4.2818)	(-4.1847)	(-3.9061)
PP	-7.8881(2.5829)	-9.3985	-6.8771	-7.5727	-8.5727	-6.7804	-7.0455	-5.3724	-5.1974	-4.3878
AR(1)	-.8032	-.9897	-.6786	-.7627	-.8511	-.6828	-.6857	-.8044	-.7577	-.6103
	(7.8574)	(-9.3995)	(-6.9158)	(-7.5590)	(-8.3012)	(-6.9475)	(-7.0267)	(5.4115)	(-5.1932)	(-4.4061)
Part II Serial correlation test results										
Constant model										
α	.0194	.0091	.0249	.0111	.0199	.0088	.0223	.0192	.0053	.0305
	(3.6041)	(1.3796)	(2.7931)	(2.2296)	(3.4930)	(1.0315)	(2.3208)	(2.4627)	(.7268)	(3.3172)
DW-stat	1.6048	1.9438	1.3380	1.5236	1.7022	1.3658	1.3723	1.6025	1.5108	1.2152
α	.0191	.0091	.0244	.0113	.0199	.0087	.0234	.0189	.0059	.0314
	(2.8692)	(1.3593)	(1.9540)	(1.7703)	(2.9927)	(.7252)	(1.7490)	(1.9212)	(.6214)	(2.1944)
AR(1)	.1968	.0103	.3214	.2373	.1489	.3172	.3142	.1956	.2423	.3897
	(1.9251)*	(.0981)	(3.2762)**	(2.3524)**	(1.4520)	(3.2279)***	(3.2200)***	(1.3156)	(1.6606)*	(2.8130)**
DW-stat	1.6064	1.9794	1.3572	1.5254	1.7002	1.3656	1.3752	1.6088	1.5154	1.2260

sions on whether prices reflect fully all the available information. Unlike the unit root test, serial correlation test indicates variations across the sample. Only in JSE market is the assumption of zero mean and no serial correlation satisfied. For NSE although the assumption of zero mean is satisfied serial correlation problem is present while for NISE the zero mean assumption is not satisfied yet first order serial correlation is not detected. Although in almost all the markets we cannot accept that stock prices reflect fully the available information, the size of the ρ show significant variations across the market on the level of dispersion from the efficiency frontier. Positive serial correlation implies stock prices are predictable in the short-run. Market ranking with ρ shows JSE, NISE and CSE taking higher ranks with low and insignificant ρ values, which imply these markets, are closer to the weak form efficient condition. NSE, GSE and BSE take the last three positions respectively thus we cannot accept weak form efficiency in these markets.

These results tend to reflect the level of institutional development. For example, JSE has a more advanced trading technology compared to the NISE (which has recently automated its trading cycle) and the NSE (which is still in the process of mounting the CDS). JSE has also made progress in tightening the regulatory system to enhance transparency and gain investors' confidence and these may be attributable to the enhanced market efficiency, especially with implied reduced information asymmetry problems. Although ESE uses screen trading and has automated the trading cycle, it is yet to tighten the regulatory framework. MSE ranks fifth despite the progress made in modernising the trading system as these changes have recently been introduced. GSE and BSE are new markets in the process of strengthening their institutional set up.

Mean reversion test using the VAR model cover only three markets, namely the JSE, the NISE and the NSE due to data problems. Table 4 reports these test results. Unit root test results show that *LOGCPI* is I(1) while cointegration test results indicate the existence of a long-term relationship between *LOGINDEX* and *LOGCPI*. Impulse response results for the JSE show tremendous decline of *LOGINDEX* in response to stock price innovations during the first 8 periods; from .0558 in period 1 to .0076 in period 7 and $-.0004$ in period 8. Then a gradual increase is indicated to an almost constant level after the 25th period of .0033. The CPI shocks have a long-run effect on stock prices: there is an increase in stock prices to a peak of .0057 reported after a period of 1.5 years and an almost constant level after the 29th period of .002.

The results relating to the NISE also show a declining trend of *LOGINDEX* to stock prices disturbances from .0472 in period 1 to .0013 in period 9 and −.0222 in period 20. The trend is reversed in 1.9 years period and an almost constant level is gained after the 28th period of −.015. In response to CPI disturbances, stock prices increase from .003 to .0466, which is a 15 times rise in the first 15 periods. This declines to .038 in the 3-year period and remains almost constant at this level.

The NSE shows a volatile response to stock price shocks in the first 16 periods while an almost constant response is indicated after the 27th period of .005. In response to CPI shocks, stock returns increase 4 folds by the 10th period, then decline to .027 by the end of two years.

Variance decomposition results capture the non-stationary component for both *LOGINDEX* and *LOGCPI*. The results reported in Table 4 show variations in the proportionate size of non-stationary component and the timing of the reversal effect differ across the markets. For the JSE an S-shaped response curve is indicated with the proportion of temporary component increasing from about 5% to 23.6% in the first 11 periods. It gains a peak in 29th period of 24.6% and then declines slowly. The implication is that CPI shocks contribute significantly to changes in stock prices in the short run; the stock prices also respond significantly to own shocks. In the long run, stock price shocks are dominant implying short-lived non-stationary component of the stock prices. This may explain why the serial correlation and unit root tests fail to detect the autocorrelation in the series giving results that show stock prices are efficient in JSE market.

The non-stationary component for the NISE also shows an S-shaped response, but the impact takes a longer time to fade away. The NSE portrays a quadratic curvature, increasing at a faster rate initially and then increasing at a declining rate, but never actually declining to zero.

Overall, therefore, the significant impact of CPI shocks on stock prices suggests that stock prices have a significant non-stationary component, which rules out the possibility that stock returns are pure random walk processes even in the more advanced markets.

Comparative Analysis of Efficiency of the 'Before' and 'After' Periods Across the Markets

Market Response to the Trading System Reforms

We consider gains in efficiency by comparing the period 'before' and 'after' the reforms. For the trading system we capture the shift to open out-cry trading system in the NSE in November 1991; and the automation of the trading cycle in the NISE in April 1997; introduction of

TABLE 4. Test for Market Efficiency Using the VAR Model

This table reports the mean reversion results using VAR model. LLH is the log-likelihood statistic from the cointegration test results. Variance decomposition reports results for *LOGINDEX* in relation to the CPI shocks, thus the permanent component. Parentheses of variance decomposition results are standard errors. JSE = Johannesburg stock exchange; NISE = Nigeria Stock Exchange; NSE = Nairobi Stock Exchange. Levels of statistical significance are defined as * = (10%); ** = (5%); *** = (1%) for all tables

	JSE	NISE	NSE
Unit root test			
LCPI			
ADF	−2.0862(−2.5879)	−1.9494(−3.1629)	−.2673(−2.5903)
AR(1)	−.0092(−2.0862)	−.0288(−1.9494)	−.0046(−.2673)
Trend		−.00012(−.3727)	
PP	−2.2963(−2.5879)	−1.9668(3.1629)	−.8462(−2.5882)
AR(1)	−.0121(−2.8078)	−.0320(−2.1387)	−.0125(−.7957)
Trend		−.00024(−.8434)	
Cointegration results			
C	5.5159	.1.3500	−1.3262
LCPI	.7622(2.1031)**	1.7828(11.8128)***	1.7583(5.2524)***
LLH	366.2373	299.9812	317.8385
Trend		.01289	
Variance decomposition			
6	4.8601(.0768)	2.9141(.0855)	17.8012(.0763)
12	23.6942(.1177)	37.1924(.1085)	51.5187(.1032)
24	24.4027(.1185)	69.3186(.2000)	72.6059(.1429)
36	24.5812(.1195)	75.2341(.2457)	80.1178(.1729)
48	24.5262(.1203)	78.2132(.2847)	84.0023(.1984)

the central depository system in January 1997 and the commencement of daily trading in November 1997 for MSE; commencement of manual centralised clearing and settlement in April 1996 for GSE; the introduction of computerised trading system in February 1995 for ESE and the shift to automated electronic trading in JSE in June 1996. We infer positive gains in the 'after' period if the value of *RHO* is lower than the 'before' period. The test results are reported in Table 5.

The results for the NSE show a shift from long run predictability to short run predictability in the post reform period though the zero mean assumption is satisfied. When we consider the average absolute value of ρ a significant decline is indicated from .4461 in the 'before' period to .2792 in the 'after' period. To capture the implications of other reforms implemented during the period we calculated the average value of ρ in the post reform period with and without the licensing of additional brokerage firms in June 1994. Our results show a decline in average value of ρ to .2152 before the expansion of brokerage firms implying a signifi-

TABLE 5. Market Response to Changes in the Trading System

This table analyses the response of market efficiency to changes in trading system testing for presence of serial correlation in the 'before' and 'after' period and average the size of coefficient ρ

NSE response to introduction of open outcry trading system November 1991.		
	1988:01-1991:10	1991:11-1999:12
α DW	.0051(1.1993) 2.4400	.0091(1.0917) 1.3653
α AR(1)	.0049(1.4101) −.2243(−1.5100)*	.0092(.7861) .3172(3.6203)**
Average value of ρ in the period and the mean difference test results using the t-ratio	.4461	.2762
	t-ratio = 2.38(.019)	

NISE response to introduction of automation of the trading cycle in April 1997.		
	1988:01-1997:04	1997:05-1999:12
α DW	.0334(9.7092)*** 1.6157	−.0160(−1.6171) 2.8173
α AR (1)	.0348(8.0135)*** .1885(1.9999)*	−.0160(−2.4783)** −.4159(−2.5037)**
Average value of ρ in the period and the mean difference test results using the t-ratio	.2685	.3255
	t-ratio = 2.49(.015)	

JSE response to automation of trading system in June 1996		
	1988:01-1996:06	1996:07-1999:12
α DW	.0146(2.9696)** 2.1199	.0052(.4159) 1.9676
α AR (1)	.0151(3.2302)** −.0645(−.6431)	.0051(.4136) −.0155(−.0953)
Average value of ρ in the period and the mean difference test results using the t-ratio	.2117	.0392
	t-ratio = 9.35(.000)	

MSE response to introduction of CDS in January 1997		
	1991:07-1997:01	1997:02-1999:12
α DW	.0126(2.0807)** 1.4141	.0051(.7250) 1.7970
α AR (1)	.0139(1.6808)* .2840(2.3909)**	.0052(.6583) .0903(.5158)
Average value of ρ in the period and the mean difference test results using the t-ratio	.2355	.2471
	t-ratio = 1.15(.254)	

TABLE 5 (continued)

GSE response to commencement of manual centralised clearing and settlement in April 1996		
	1990:12-1996:04	1996:05-1999:12
α DW	.0236(2.2875)* 1.3917	.0164(1.2975) 1.1841
α AR (1)	.0265(1.8920)* .2880(2.4019)**	.0151(.7702) .4009(2.8465)**
Average value of ρ in the period and the mean difference test results using the t-ratio	.2726	.3099
	t-ratio = 3.36(.001)	
ESE response to introduction of computerised trading system February 1995		
	1992:02-1995:02	1995:03-1999:12
α DW	.0223(3.0744)** 1.8257	.0175(2.3251)* 1.5215
α AR (1)	.0218(2.6778)* .0741(.4272)	.0177(1.8214)* .2386(1.8457)*
Average value of ρ in the period and the mean difference test results using the t-ratio	.1316	.1796
	t-ratio = 2.51(.017)	

cant gain in efficiency (t-$ratio$ = 4.16(.000)). Thus we conclude that the expansion of brokerage industry failed to sustain the immediate gains realised from change in trading system.

The NISE results show significant long-run predictability of stock return in the 'after' period as compared to the 'before' when short-run predictability is reported. The average value of ρ increases in the post-period with the introduction of automated trade cycle. Interestingly, while in the 'before' period the assumption of zero mean is not satisfied, in the 'after' period this assumption is satisfied, fulfilling one of the conditions for random walk hypothesis.

JSE phased out floor trading in June 1996. Our results show the random walk hypothesis satisfied in the 'after' period, the decline in ρ value indicating gains in market efficiency. We traced the response of the market to various changes implemented in the post reform period to capture the relationship between changing the trading system and tightening of regulatory system in 1997. The p value declined from .0621 in the 'before' reform period to .0598 in the period after the introduction of electronic trading but before any further changes in the regulatory system. Gains in efficiency were enhanced when Stock Exchange News Services (SENS)[17] was introduced in 1997 and insider trading law tightened in 1999; the average value of p declined to .0264. Thus, we conclude that though changes in trading system show gains in efficiency, further gains are realised when regulatory system is tightened to protect the right of investors.

For the MSE the introduction of the CDS trading system and daily trading also saw the random walk hypotheses satisfied. Comparing MSE and JSE we find similar results in the 'after' period though the 'before' periods are different; MSE shows short run predictability in the 'before' period.

In GSE manual centralised clearing and settlement was introduced in April 1996 aimed to minimise trade failures and strengthen the level of co-ordination between the brokers and the registrar. However this reform was not enough to facilitate gains in efficiency. For both the 'before' and 'after' period positive serial correlation is significant, and the level of inefficiency is significantly higher in the 'after' period. Introduction of a computerised trading system in ESE did not show significant gains in the short run. In the transition process, the market fails to satisfy the assumptions of random walk hypothesis and the situation deteriorates in the 'after' period.

When we compare the average values of p across the markets we find that low level of efficiency is realised with trading system that have advanced their trading technology. For example, significant difference is indicated between GSE without electronic system (p = .3099), and ESE, which has automated trading system (p = .1796) together with MSE, which has started the automation (p = .2471). JSE with more advanced trading technology has a value of p equal to .0431 and compared to NSE, which is preparing for automation trading (p = .2741). These results imply that there are positive gains investing in trading technology as this reduces the transaction costs by quickening the settlement process. In addition the regulatory system must be tightened to protect the rights of investors thus help to build their confidence with the market.

Market Response to Changes in Regulatory System

The analysis of changes in the regulatory system covers only JSE and GSE markets because of data constraint in other markets; Table 6 re-

TABLE 6. Response of the Markets to Foreign Investors' Participation

We analyse the relaxation of restrictions on foreign investors participation in ZSE, MSE, NISE and NSE testing for presence of serial correlation in the 'before' and 'after' period and average the size of coefficient ρ

ZSE response to entry of foreign investors in 1993		
	1988:01-1993:04	1993:05-1999:12
α DW	.0104(1.1890) .8562	.0341(3.3017)** 1.4765
α AR (1)	.0118(.6828) .5733(5.4960)***	.0342(2.5342)* .2552(2.3260)*
Average value of ρ in the period and the mean difference test results using the t-ratio	.4897	.4739
	t-ratio = .72(.476)	
NSE response to entry of foreign investors in 1995		
	1988:01-1994:12	1995:01-1999:12
α DW	.0217(2.5267)* 1.1162	−.0114(−1.7528)* 1.6645
α AR (1)	.0241(1.7017)* .4346(3.9863)***	−.0121(−1.8418) −.0964(−.9101)
Average value of ρ in the period and the mean difference test results using the t-ratio	.0048	.0045
	t-ratio = .13(.896)	
NISE response to further relaxation of the foreign investors regulations		
	1988:01-1994:12	1995:01-1999:12
α DW	.0295(11.6521)*** 1.0598	.0144(1.6777)* 1.8153
α AR(1)	.0302(7.1709)*** .4621(4.7023)***	.0144(1.5115) .0932(.7140)
Average value of ρ in the period and the mean difference test results using the t-ratio	.2957	.2626
	t-ratio = 1.41(.162)	
MSE response to foreign investors entry		
	1991:07-1994:12	1995:01-1999:12
α DW	.0264(3.6666)*** 1.7215	−.0014(−.2442) 1.5826
α AR(1)	.0283(3.4797)*** .1104(.708)	−.0014(−.2044) .2060(1.6129)
Average value of ρ in the period and the mean difference test results using the t-ratio	.2153	.2553
	t-ratio = 2.73(.009)	

ports the results. JSE launched a big shake up of the market with the Stock Exchange Amendment Act September 1995 implemented since November 1995. In the 'after' period our results show that both the zero mean and *IID* assumption of random walk hypothesis are satisfied, implying a market that is more efficient and ready to facilitate enhancement of market liquidity. Tracing the response of the market to the various changes implemented we find the value of ρ reducing from .2232 in the period before the reforms to .0605 (*t-ratio* = 8.51(.000)) in the reform period before the introduction of SENS and then to .0264 (*t-ratio* = 12.23(.000)) with the introduction of SENS and tightening of the insider law in 1999. For GSE market the introduction of SEC saw no significant gains in efficiency, which may be explained partially by the loss in efficiency realised with the change in trading system. Before the change in trading system, insignificant gains were indicated with the SEC.

Market Response to Relaxation of Foreign Investors' Participation

To analyse the response of the markets to increased participation by foreign investors, we consider the relationship between the efficiency level of the market and the relaxation for foreign investors' participation and also the period before and after relaxation of foreign investors' participation. To analyse the 'before' and 'after' periods, we consider the NISE (which further relaxed the controls on foreign investors' participation in January 1995), the ZSE (which opened the market to foreign investors in April 1993), and the NSE January 1995. Table 7 reports the response of the markets to foreign investors' participation. ZSE show no significant gains with the entry of foreign investors; in fact in the 'after' period random walk hypotheses are rejected. In addition, an increase in expected returns is indicated in the 'after' period an indication that investors were demanding higher returns because of increased market risk. Both GSE and MSE show a decline in market efficiency; the value of ρ increase in the 'after' period though the zero mean assumption is satisfied. NSE shows significant gain with the entry of foreign investors; the significance and level of serial correlation improved tremendously. The average ρ declines from .3569 in the 'before' period to .2952 in the 'after' period. The NISE shows lower returns and efficiency gains in the period 'after' the reforms, which widened the participation level of foreign investors. Lower return may be interpreted as an

TABLE 7. Market Response to Changes in the Regulatory System

JSE response to the SEC Act 1995		
	1988:01-1995:11	1995:12-1999:12
α DW	.0142(2.7476)*** 2.1176	.0073(.6731) 1.9760
α AR(1)	.0147(2.9897)** $-.0641(-.6150)$	.0073(.6719) $-.0120(-.0802)$
Average value of ρ in the period and the mean difference test results using the t-ratio	.2232	.0424
	t-ratio = 9.37(.000)	
Mean difference in average in the reform period with and without SENS		
Before the reform	Reform period without SENS	Reform period with SENS
1988:01-1995:11[a]	1995:12-1997:10[b]	1997:11-1999:12[c]
.2231	.0605	.0264
t-ratio test for the mean differences between: a-b; t-ratio = 8.51(.000) b-c; t-ratio = 12.23(.000)		
GSE response to the introduction of SEC1993		
	1990:12-1993:12	1994:01-1999:12
α DW	.0147(1.2648) 2.1695	.0238(2.2629)** 1.0413
α AR(1)	.0173(1.6619) $-.1172(-.7120)$	.0231(1.3005) .4789(4.5559)***
Average value of ρ in the period and the mean difference test results using the t-ratio	.2757	.2939
	t-ratio = 1.04(.307)	
Mean difference in average in the reform period with and without trading system		
Before SEC	SEC without trading system changes	SEC with trading system
1990:12-1993:12[a]	1994:01-1996:04[b]	1996:05-1999:12[c]
.2757	.2687	.3099
t-ratio test for the mean differences between: a-b; t-ratio = .35(.725) b-c; t-ratio = 3.72(.000)		

indication that domestic firms are able to access investment funds at lower costs (see Kim and Singal, 2000).

Ranking the five market by the average absolute value of ρ coefficient and the participation of foreign investors we find MSE takes the highest rank with a value of $\rho = .2553$ while NISE takes a second position with $\rho = .2626$; the marginal difference is very minimal and both markets allow 100% foreign participation. GSE and ZSE take the last positions with values of $\rho = .3042$ and $.4739$. In both markets the allowed level of foreign investors' participation is less than 100%. These results imply that relaxation of foreign investors' participation in portfolio investment has positive gains in addition to other institutional reforms especially when the proportionate participation is high.

Overall, therefore, our results show that there are positive gains in terms of market efficiency when stock exchanges adopt advanced trading technology aimed to reduce transaction costs and settlement periods. Also positive gains are realised when the regulatory system is strengthened to reduce information asymmetry problem and protect the rights of investors, and when controls on foreign investors' participation in the market are relaxed.

Test Results for Volatility

Comparative Analysis of Volatility Across the Markets

We analyse the volatility structure for individual markets using GARCH-type model and compare across the markets and also between the 'before' and 'after' reform periods. For markets that indicate no ARCH effects, a squared residuals measure is used, while the GARCH-type method is used for markets which have an adequate data sample and which exhibit clustering effects. Table 8 provides results for the estimated GARCH models.

The analysis of the volatility of individual markets covers the JSE, MSE, NSE, NISE, ESE and ZSE. The returns for JSE show no serial correlation and heteroscedasticity problems as indicated by the autocorrelation function results (AC(1) $-.014(.902)$; AC(6) $-.001(.487)$; AC(12) $-.020(.462)$) and the ARCH-LM test results ($\text{Resid}^2_{(t-1)} = -.0355(.2924)$; F-stat $= .0855(.7708)$). Thus, we do not use the GARCH-type models; rather we use squared standard deviations from a recursive regression of a constant return model to obtain a proxy for *ex-ante* volatility. We tested for the significance of volatility persistence by regress-

TABLE 8. GARCH Model Results

NSEF is a dummy variable that takes the value of one if the market opens to foreign investors in the market and zero otherwise; $AC(n)$ is the autocorrelation function at lag n where $n=1,2,3,4....$; R_{t-i} are the lagged returns; $MA(q)$ is the moving average process; LLH is the log likelihood; *ASYM* is a dummy variable equal to one when returns are negative and 0 otherwise; *DUMSIL* is a dummy variable that takes the value of one for the period with the SEC and zero otherwise.

	NISE	ZSE	NSE	ESE	GSE
Autocorrelation function results for stock returns					
AC(1)	.167(.043)	.362(.000)	.289(.000)	.197(.052)	.335(.000)
AC(6)	.107(.000)	.196(.000)	.200(.000)	.184(.135)	.079(.079)
AC(12)	.040(.000)	−.064(.000)	.032(.000)	−.106(.273)	−.038(.111)
AC(24)	−.111(.000)	−.167(.000)	−.014(.004)	.037(.063)	−.028(.301)
OLS estimation results, dealing with the identified problem of serial correlation					
C	.0132(2.9621)**	.0102(1.5261)	.0222(2.5634)*	.0284(2.7260)***	.0070(2.4993)**
$R_{(t-1)}$	.1132(1.4054)	.2948(3.8237)***	.6424(3.6344)***	.1497(1.663)*	−.0237(−.2577)
$R_{(t-2)}$	.3224(4.0044)***		−.6852(−4.7987)***	−.6072(−3.443)***	.8396(8.9428)***
$R_{(t-3)}$		.3175(4.0842)***			
NSEF			−.0332(−2.5458)**		−.0050(−1.8356)*
DUMSIL					
MA(1)			−.3966(−1.8887)*	.7979(5.6412)***	.3160(2.6888)*
MA(2)			.4739(2.5808)**		−.8848(−11.0663)***
MA(3)					−.4040(−4.2860)***
R^2	.1291	.2276	.1779	.0945	.1782
Adj R^2	.1165	.2163	.1475	.0639	.1289
LLH	240.4902	166.5099	188.8269	146.3785	125.7161
Autocorrelation function, testing for serial correlation from the OLS estimation above					
AC(1)	−.047(.549)	−.001(.990)	.079(.584)	.033(.743)	.023(.811)
AC(6)	.035(.687)	.080(.864)	.030(.275)	.137(.690)	.028(.862)
AC(12)	−.031(.959)	.005(.314)	−.042(.360)	−.088(.888)	−.023(.980)
AC(24)	−.091(.824)	−.038(.035)	−.035(.887)	.038(.663)	−.047(.901)
ARCH-LM test results for heteroscedasticity problem					
C	.0010(2.0169)	.0043(5.3735)***	.0025(2.2787)*	.0016(2.5033)*	.0036(2.1662)**
Resid(−1)	.5333(7.4065)***	.2059(2.4656)*	.3791(4.8133)***	−.0241(−.2452)	.3534(3.8536)***
Resid(−2)				.3820(3.8800)***	
F-stat	54.8563(.000)	6.0793(.0149)*	23.1679(.0000)	7.6018(.0009)	14.8505(.0002)

Estimation results for the GARCH model

GARCH					
C	-2.6810(-4.9567)***	.0170(2.3284)**	.8807(1.9164)*	.0092(1.6822)*	.0089(.8418)
$R_{(t-1)}$	.0122(4.4107)***	.3539(4.2496)***	.0091(1.4352)	.3276(4.0660)***	-.1402(-.3700)
$R_{(t-2)}$	.5506(24.7210)***		.5822(3.7634)***	.1167(.4584)	.5905(1.7925)*
$R_{(t-3)}$	.1199(2.5317)*	.2967(3.6271)***	-.7612(-11.1563)***		
NSEF			-.0234(-2.9324)**		-.0093(-.7429)
DUMSIL			-.4312(-2.1096)**	.0588(.8238)	.5353(1.4307)
MA(1)			.5990(5.6173)***		-.4960(-1.0485)
MA(2)					-.2983(-1.9804)*
MA(3)					
C	.0012(11.2872)**	.0001(1.7298)*	.0011(5.4654)***	.0003(3.1228)**	.0014(4.7764)***
ARCH1	.5275(7.7514)***	.0950(1.2370)	.9723(4.3761)***	.1914(2.0517)	.9768(5.0938)***
GARCH1	-.4814(-4.6350)***	.7702(7.5814)***	-.0486(-1.8410)*	-.4844(-4.0604)***	-.0465(-1.9064)*
ASYM		.0022(1.6662)*	1.49E-05(.0603)	.8299(8.8293)***	
R^2	.0591	.2159	.2137	.0201	.1208
Adj R^2	.1070	.1805	.1532	-.0606	.0392
LLH	284.2343	187.0656	235.6947	162.8786	161.6454

ARCH-LM test for any more heteroscedasticity problem

C	1.0176(3.1748)***	1.0032(6.8847)***	1.0882(5.5622)***	1.1838(5.0564)***	.9751(4.2438)***
Std resid(-1)	.0453(.5332)	-.0039(.0454)	-.0477(-.5609)	-.0818(-.7769)	.0866(.8868)
F-stat	.2843(.5947)	.0021(.9638)	.3146(.5758)	.6036(.4392)	.7864(.3722)

Unit root test for the GARCH volatility	-4.7207(-2.5779)	-2.3172(-2.5780)	-4.7375(-2.5779)	-3.2434(-2.5836)	-4.3476(-2.5816)

Summary statistics for the GARCH volatility

Mean	.0015	.0056	.0046	.0002	.0070
Median	.0009	.0050	.0013	.0017	.0018
Maximum	.0301	.0158	.1374	.0137	.1390
Minimum	7.54E-07	.0003	5.74E-05	3.30E-06	2.97E-05
Std Deviation	.0031	.0036	.0131	.0020	.0184
Skewness	6.9084	.3208	7.9501	2.9885	5.1705
Kurtosis	56.3667	2.1475	76.3274	15.5874	32.0850
JB	17853.6	6.6399	33074.59	752.3968	4248.235
Probability	.000000	.03615	.00000	.0000	.0000

ing stock prices on the lagged values of estimated volatility. The results show a negative and significant result implying that volatility is persistent (*coefficient* = −1.6809; *t-ratio* = −1.7325(.0878)). To confirm the significance of volatility persistency we estimate a GARCH-type model and the lagged GARCH variable was positive and significant (*coefficient* = .5450; *t-ratio* = 1.7810(.0794)) while the ARCH variable was not significant (*coefficient* = .3792; *t-ratio* = 1.2747(.2068)). We however confirm volatility persistency in JSE, which implies the volatility impacts on stock prices. As noted by Choudhry (1996) a significant impact of volatility on stock prices can only take place if shocks to volatility are persistent and not transitory. The market will not make an adjustment to future discount rate if shocks to volatility are not permanent. Returns for MSE also did not show significant serial correlation problem especially at higher levels; (AC(1) −.237(.015); AC(6) −.033(.071); AC(12) −.040(.232)); ARCH-test did not confirm any heteroscedasticity problem either. We applied the same methodology as in JSE to analyse volatility and found volatility is persistent.

Correlogram and ARCH-LM test results for ESE, NISE, ZSE, and NSE show presence of volatility clustering thus we use GARCH-type model to study volatility in these markets. The results reported in Table 8 shows some differences in volatility structure across the market that does not seem to reflect the institutional development of the market. For example, although both NSE and NISE show significant time varying premium the implied behaviour of investors varies. Time varying premium is negative in NISE suggesting that investors are risk lovers while in NSE it is positive implying risk-averse investors. Asymmetric response is indicated in ZSE, NSE and ESE markets where the positive signs indicate that volatility is higher with bad news.[18] Uniformly across the markets, volatility is persistent and clustering. Conditional variance coefficient values add up to less than one implying that volatility is not explosive while the unit root test implies that volatility is stable. With no more unexplained structures, we conclude that a martingale random process defines the stock prices.

We compare magnitude of volatility across the markets using the mean value calculated in summary statistics for normality test. GSE and NSE report the highest mean values of volatility, which in addition have high degree of dispersion. ESE has the lowest value of volatility and also lowest degree of dispersion. Although MSE has a relatively low volatility level, it has a high degree of dispersion while for ZSE volatility is high but closer to normal distribution.

Amihud et al. (1990) explain a relationship between volatility and market efficiency where efficiency in price discovery process is associated with low volatility making prices more informative. We compared our volatility results with the efficiency results reported in the foregoing section. A casual observation of the results indicates that the lowly ranked market by level of efficiency have higher volatility than markets indicated to be more efficient. We used granger causality test to see the direction of relation. We found JSE, MSE, NISE and ZSE have bi-directional causality between market efficiency and volatility. It implies a feedback effect where, for example, high volatility is followed by low efficiency and the later feeding back to volatility. Thus, any reform targeted to reduce volatility is likely to be followed by gains in market efficiency and this feeds back to reduce volatility. For ESE, GSE and NSE, a unidirectional causality from volatility to efficiency is indicated. These results imply that any efforts targeted to increase market efficiency will not necessarily see reduced market efficiency.

Comparative Analysis of Volatility for 'Before' and 'After' Period of Reforms Across the Markets

Market Response to Trading System Reforms

With regard to changes in the trading system, both GSE and MSE show similar direction of relationship between efficiency and volatility. For GSE, significant reduction in market efficiency is associated with insignificant decline in volatility, while in MSE, both volatility and efficiency show insignificant decline. These imply that if significant gains in efficiency are to follow, then volatility must decline significantly. For NISE and ESE, significant increase in volatility is associated with significant decline in efficiency, while NSE show insignificant increase in efficiency with rise in volatility.

Market Response to Changes in Regulatory System

The regulatory changes introduced by JSE in 1995 saw an insignificant rise in volatility from .0025 to .0058 (*t-ratio* = 1.17(.247)). The reform period before the introduction of SENS saw a decline in volatility to .0015, while the reform period with the SENS saw volatility increase to .0094. For GSE, there was also an insignificant increase in volatility from .0068 to .0070 (*t-ratio* = .04(.964)).

Market Response of the Relaxation Foreign Investors' Participation

The entry of foreign investors shows mixed results while the level of volatility tends to reflect the level of foreign investors' participation. For example, ZSE reports a significantly high volatility with the entry of foreign investors, increasing from .0041 to .0068 (t-$ratio$ = 4.31(.000)). Given the granger causality relation, we conclude that as long as the market is volatile, distortions in price discovery process will be reflected. NSE indicate insignificant decline in volatility from .0048 to .0045 (t-$ratio$ = .13(.896)). This implies that slight decline in volatility would see a significant gain in efficiency. NISE show a significant increase from .0010 to .0023 (t-$ratio$ = 2.26 (.028)), which implies that there is need for significant decline in volatility if significant market efficiency is to be achieved.

Overall, therefore, more efficient markets have lower volatility than less efficient markets. However, this study finds no evidence that the structure of market volatility is dictated by the institutional structure. For example, all the sample markets show significant volatility persistence and clustering, while leverage effect and the pricing of time varying premium vary across the markets.

CONCLUSION

In this paper, we investigate the response of emerging stock markets in Africa to various reforms implemented during the revitalising process capturing mainly market efficiency and volatility. We identify three main types of reforms, namely the strengthening of the regulatory framework, shifts in trading system and adoption of modern trading technology, and relaxation of restrictions on the participation of foreign investors. Basing on a selective review of the literature, we invoke market microstructure theory in order to provide a tractable framework for studying the response of the emerging stock markets in Africa to the reform process.

We cannot conclude for weak form efficiency in all the market although markets with strengthened institutional base tend to show lesser inefficiency. Random walk hypothesis is not satisfied in all the markets except JSE, but even for JSE the presence of non-stationary component makes us conclude that returns in the market are not pure random walk processes.

In presence of high volatility, reforms in trading system show insignificant gains. However, a comparative analysis across the markets shows that modernised trading systems are less inefficient. More gains in trading system are indicated when such reforms are coupled with tightened protection of investors, as indicated by JSE results; this enhances confidence among investors.

Relaxation of restrictions on foreign investors' participation shows some positive gains in efficiency, though the magnitude varies across the markets; mixed results are indicated with volatility. Only JSE and GSE markets were analysed for changes in regulatory system. Results show more gains when regulatory system is more exhaustive.

Our results do not show a clear link between volatility structure and market institutional structure; in all markets volatility is persistent clustering. However, volatility level is related to the underlying institutional structure with a strong relationship shown between volatility and efficiency. Markets with high levels of inefficiency show high volatility. Although causality between efficiency and volatility vary across the markets, in general, reforms targeted to reduce volatility will reap higher efficiency.

Overall, we conclude that the emerging stock markets in Africa will enjoy more benefits with investments to improve the market microstructure.

NOTES

1. For example, for the Tel Aviv stock market, Amihud et al. (1997) show gains in efficiency of the price discovery process, increased liquidity and low volatility as a result of the adoption of a new trading system. Moreover, some studies suggest that the entry of foreign investors in an emerging market has been followed by increased liquidity and enhanced efficiency in the price discovery process, although market volatility has either remained unchanged or actually declined (see Richards, 1996; Kim, 1998; Kim and Singal, 2000). However, Chang et al. (1999) show no change in liquidity and efficiency of price discovery process, while volatility increased with the continuous auction system in the Taiwan stock market.

2. For example, Osei (1998) applies the serial correlation method to test for efficiency and finds that the Ghana stock market is weak form inefficient for the period 1994:05-1995:12. Parkinson (1987) also finds weak form inefficiency for the Nairobi stock market for the period 1974-1978 and by Muragu (1996) for the period 1979-1988. Inanga and Emenuga (1996) obtain similar findings for the Nigerian stock market using weekly and daily data for the period 1991 to 1994. Further econometric tests by Emenuga (1996) confirm that the Nigerian stock market is semi-strong inefficient for the period 1987:01-1991:12. Moreover, in a comparative study of the Botswana and Zimbabwe stock markets, Jefferis et al. (1999) apply the unit root test and

find that while the former is weak form inefficient, the latter is weak form efficient for the period 1989 to 1996.

3. We do not study liquidity because of serious inconsistencies in the data across the markets.

4. Casablanca Stock Exchange (CSE) in Morocco; Tunis Stock Exchange (TSE) in Tunisia, Cairo and Alexandria stock exchanges in Egypt (ESE); Zimbabwe Stock Exchange (ZSE) in Zimbabwe; Nairobi Stock Exchange (NSE) in Kenya; Nigeria Stock Exchange (NISE) in Nigeria; Mauritius Stock Exchange (MSE) in Mauritius; Botswana Stock Exchange (BSE) in Botswana; Ghana Stock Exchange (GSE) in Ghana; Swaziland Stock Exchange (SSE) in Swaziland; Namibia Stock Exchange (NASE) in Namibia; Khartoum Stock Exchange (KSE) in Sudan; Lusaka Stock Exchange (LUSE) in Zambia; Malawi Stock Exchange (MASE) in Malawi; Tanzanian Stock Exchange (TASE) in Tanzania; Uganda Stock Exchange (USE) in Uganda; and Maputo Stock Exchange (MPSE) in Mozambique.

5. The origin of the regional market dates back to 1973 when UMOEA members signed a treaty for the creation of a regional market. A regional council for public savings and financial markets was formed in October 1997 after extensive negotiations between member countries. The regional market, with headquarters in Abidjan, now includes Benin, Burkina Faso, Cote d'Ivoire, Guinea-Bissau, Mali, Niger, Senegal and Togo.

6. The Capital Market Law (Law 95/1992) allowed for the lifting of restrictions on foreign investment and abolition of capital gains taxes and taxes on dividends. Also the Law established an Arbitration Board to address grievances raised by investors.

7. JET is a centralized order driven electronic market providing for agency and principal trading in securities. Only members of the JSE are permitted to enter orders and execute transactions on the JET system prior to disclosing to their clients whether they are acting as principal or agent.

8. Investors face charges payable to the SEC and the Stock Exchange. Brokerage fee charges range between 1% and 2.5% while SEC fee is 1%. Dividend income tax is 0% in JSE, ESE and MSE; 10% in GSE, NSE, NASE and NISE and 15% in ZSE and BSE. Thus there are no significant differences between the old and new stock exchanges. In almost all the markets capital gain tax has been suspended. The NISE suspended capital gain taxes in 1997, while NSE suspended capital gain tax in 1985 in response to the recommendation of the IFC/Central bank of Kenya study report of 1984. In the GSE, capital gain tax was first exempted till November 2000. The period was extended with another five years to November 2005. For ESE capital gain tax of 2% levied on security investment in 1992 was cancelled in 1st July 1996.

9. Due to advances in information technology, most of the emerging stock markets in Africa are replacing the manual trading system with automated trading in attempt to improve liquidity and reduce the costs of trading.

10. Chang et al. (1999) and Lang and Lee (1999) show mixed results on liquidity for Taiwan stock market. While the former indicate no significant change in liquidity with the shift from call to continuous trading, the latter show a significant gain. Chang et al. (1999) also show call auction to have lower volatility compared to the continuous auction. Similarly, the call auction was indicated to be more efficient compared to the continuous system.

11. Studies testing for serial correlation use high frequency data such as daily series and weekly series taking the last observation at the end of the day or week. The implicit assumption is that stocks are frequently and therefore no prevalence of thin trading.

However, emerging markets are described as thinly traded where for example some stocks are not traded on daily or weekly basis. Thus we assume the monthly frequency captures the frequency of trading in these markets.

12. The one period ahead forecast error, which is the difference between the actual value of dependent variable and a forecast made on the basis of the independent variables and the past forecast errors.

13. This is the Cochrane (1988) variance ratio.

14. Gallagher (1995) explores various markets but the estimated stationary (permanent) component does not reflect the diversity in institutional status of the market.

15. Choudhry (1996) observes that volatility clustering could be attributed to clustering of trading volumes, nominal interest rates, dividend yield, money supply and external shocks.

16. Fraser and Power (1997) argue that at the aggregate level this would indicate that *ex post* market returns may incorporate information regarding informed agents' overall perceptions regarding economy-wide future business conditions, and such sentiments may be reflected in future market volatility.

17. SENS was introduced to provide subscribers with fast dissemination of price sensitive market information.

18. There are various arguments on the stock price response to shocks, which indicate that the relationship could take a negative or positive relationship. Nelson (1991) argues that the sign on returns influence the future volatility being negatively correlated with the direction of actual price changes. Black (1976) and Christie (1982) point out that stock returns tend to be negatively correlated with changes in volatility so that a reduction in the equity value of a firm raises its debt-to-equity ratio, hence raising the riskiness of the firm as manifested by an increase in future volatility. If returns are less than expected they tend to increase future volatility and if higher than expected they tend to decrease future return volatility. Glosten et al. (1993) observe that investors may not require a high risk premium if the risky time periods coincide with periods when investors are better able to bear particular types of risks. Again if future seems risky the investor may want to save more in the present thus lowering demand for larger premia. If it is risky to transfer income to the future and investors have no opportunity to invest in a risk-free asset, the price of a risky asset may considerably reduce the risk premium. Thus, it is possible to have a positive and a negative relationship between current returns and current variance.

REFERENCES

Aitken, B. (1998) Have institutional investors destabilised emerging markets? *Contemporary Economic Policy*, 16, 173-184

Amihud, Y., Mendelson, H. and Murgia, M. (1990) Stock market microstructure and return volatility: evidence from Italy. *Journal of Banking and Finance*, 14, 423-440

Amihud, Y., Mendelson, H. and Lauterbach, B. (1997) Market microstructure and securities values. Evidence from Tel Aviv stock exchange. *Journal of Financial Economics*, 45, 365-390

Bekart, G. and Harvey, C.R. (1997) Emerging equity market volatility. *Journal of Financial Economics*, 43, 29-77

Black, F. (1976) Studies of stock price volatility changes, proceedings of the 1976 Meeting of Business and Economic Statistics Section, American Statistical Association, 177-181

Blanchard, O.J. and Quah, D. (1989) The Dynamic effects of aggregate supply and demand disturbances. *American Economic Review*, 79, 655-73

Bollerslev, T. and Mikkelson, O.H. (1999) Long-term equity anticipation securities and stock market volatility dynamics. *Journal of Econometrics*, 92, 75-99

Bollerslev, T., Chou, R.Y. and Kroner, F.K. (1992) ARCH modelling in Finance: A review of the theory and empirical evidence. *Journal of Econometrics*, 52, 5-59

Caprio, G., Jr., and Demirgüç-Kunt, A. (1998) The role of long term finance: Theory and evidence. *The World Bank Research Observer*, 13(2), 171-189

Chang, R.P., Hsu, S., Huang, N. and Rhee, S.G. (1999) The effects of trading methods on volatility and liquidity: evidence from Taiwan Stock Exchange. *Journal of Business Finance and Accounting*, 26(1/2), 137-170

Choudhry, T. (1996) Stock market volatility and the crash of 1987: evidence from six emerging markets. *Journal of International Money and Finance*, 15(6), 969-981

Christie, A. (1982) The stochastic behaviour of common stock variance: Value, leverage, and interest rate effects. *Journal of Financial Economics*, 10, 407-432

Cochrane, J.H. (1988) How big is the random walk in GNP? *Journal of Political Economy*, 96, 893-920

Comerton-Forde, C. (1999) Do trading rules impact on market efficiency? A comparison of opening procedures on Australian and Jakarta stock exchanges. *Pacific-Basin Finance Journal*, 7, 495-521

Demirgüç-Kunt, A. and Levine, R. (1996) Stock market development and financial intermediaries. Stylised facts. *The World Bank Economic Review*, 10(2), 341-69

Emenuga, C. (1996) Macroeconomic factors and returns on equities: evidence from the Nigerian capital market, in *African Capital Markets Contemporary Issues*. Edited by Sam Mensah, Rector Press, 86-96

Engel, R. (1982) Autoregressive conditional heteroscedasticity with estimates of variables of UK inflation. *Econometrica*, 50, 987-1008

Fama, E.F. (1970) Efficient capital markets: A review of theory and empirical work. *Journal of Finance*, 25(2), 383-423

Fama, E.F. and French, K.R. (1988) Permanent and temporary components of stock prices. *Journal of Political Economy*, 96, 246-273

Fraser, P. and Power, D. (1997) Stock return volatility and information: An empirical analysis of Pacific Rim, UK and US equity markets. *Applied Financial Economics*, 7, 241-253

Gallagher, L.A. (1999) A multi-country analysis of the temporary and permanent components of stock prices. *Applied Financial Economics*, 9, 129-142

Garman, M.B. (1976) Market microstructure. *Journal of Financial Economics*, 3, 257-275

Glosten, L.R., Jaganathan, R. and Runkle, R.D. (1993) On the relation between the expected value and volatility of nominal excess return on stocks, *Journal of Finance*, 48, 1779-1801

Green, C.J., Maggioni, P. and Murinde, V. (2000) Regulatory lessons for emerging stock markets from a century of evidence on transaction costs and share price volatility in London Stock Exchange. *Journal of Banking and Finance*, 24, 577-601

Inanga, I.L. and Emenuga, C. (1995) Institutional, traditional, and asset pricing characteristics of the Nigerian Stock Exchange. *African Economic Research,* Consortium Research Paper No. 60

Jefferis, K.R. and Okeahalam, C.C. (1999) International stock market linkages in Southern Africa. *South African Journal of Accounting and Research*, 13(2), 27-51

Khambata, D. (2000) Impact of foreign investment on volatility and growth of emerging stock market. *Multinational Business Review*, 8, 50-59

Kim, E.H. and Singal, V. (2000) Stock market openings: Experience of emerging economies. *Journal of Business*, 73(1), 25-66

Kim, E.H. (1998) Globalisation of capital markets and Asian crises. *Journal of Applied Corporate Finance*, 1(Fall), 30-39

Koutmos, G. (1999) Asymmetric price and volatility adjustment in emerging Asian stock markets. *Journal of Business Finance and Accounting*, 26(1/2), 83-101

Kumar, P.C. and Tsetsekos, G.P. (1999) The differentiation of emerging equity markets. *Applied Financial Economics*, 9, 443-453

Lang, L.H.P. and Lee, Y.T. (1999) Performance of various transaction frequencies under call: The Case of Taiwan. *Pacific-Basin Finance Journal*, 7, 23-39

Madhavan, A. (1992) Trading mechanisms in securities markets. *Journal of Finance*, XLVII(2), 607-641

Majnoni, G. and Massa, M. (2001) Stock exchange reforms and market efficiency: the Italian experience. *European Financial Management*, 7(1), 93-115

Muragu, K. (1996) Pricing efficiency of Nairobi Stock Exchange, in *African Capital Markets Contemporary Issues*. Edited by Sam Mensah, Rector Press, 142-160

Nelson, D. (1991) Conditional heteroscedasticity in asset returns: a new approach. *Econometrica*, 59, 347-70

Osei, K.A. (1998) Analysis of factors affecting the development of an emerging capital market: the case of Ghana stock market. *African Economic Research,* Consortium Research Paper No. 76

Pagano, M. and Röell, A. (1996) Transparency and liquidity. A comparison of auction and dealer markets with informed trading. *Journal of Finance* LI(2), 579-611.

Parkinson, J.M. (1987) The EMH and the CAPM on the Nairobi Stock Exchange. *East African Economic Review*, 3(2), 105-110

Richards, A.J. (1996) Volatility and predictability in national stock markets: how do emerging and mature markets differ? *IMF Staff Papers*, 43(3), 461-501

Röell, A. (1992) Comparing the performance of stock exchange trading systems. In The Internationalisation of Capital Markets and the Regulatory Response, Fingleton, J. and D. Schoenmaker (eds), London: Graham & Trotman.

Summers, L.H. (1986) Does the stock market rationally reflect fundamental values? *Journal of Finance*, XLI(3), 591-602

Evidence on the Determinants of Capital Structure of Non-Financial Corporates in Mauritius

Ronny Manos
Clairette Ah-Hen

SUMMARY. This paper utilises the most comprehensive database on non-financial listed companies in Mauritius, to empirically study the determinants of capital structure of these firms. A model, which predicts the main determinants of leverage, is tested on a sample of 24 firms using the panel procedure over the period 1992-2000. The findings from the random effects specification appear to support the pecking order theory and to reject the trade off theory of capital structure. Further, the small role played by the Mauritian capital market as a source of long-term finance is evident from the results with respect to a number of the explanatory variables including age, growth, risk, and profitability. The strong and positive results for the size variable are consistent with the findings

---

Ronny Manos is affiliated with the Department of Economics, Loughborough Universities, Leicestershire, LE11 3TU, UK (E-mail: R.Manos@lboro.ac.uk).

Clairette Ah-Hen is affiliated with the Department of Finance and Accounting, Faculty of Law and Management, University of Mauritius, Reduit, Mauritius.

This paper was presented at the Development & Business Finance: Policy & Experience in Developing Countries, University of Manchester, 5-6 April 2001.

[Haworth co-indexing entry note]: "Evidence on the Determinants of Capital Structure of Non-Financial Corporates in Mauritius." Manos, Ronny, and Clairette Ah-Hen. Co-published simultaneously in *Journal of African Business* (International Business Press, an imprint of The Haworth Press, Inc.) Vol. 4, No. 2, 2003, pp. 129-154; and: *African Business Finance and Development Policy* (eds: Victor Murinde and Atsede Woldie) International Business Press, an imprint of The Haworth Press, Inc., 2003, pp. 129-154. Single or multiple copies of this article are available for a fee from The Haworth Document Delivery Service [1-800-HAWORTH, 9:00 a.m. - 5:00 p.m. (EST). E-mail address: docdelivery@haworthpress.com].

of other studies and with the trade off theory, but are at odds with the general findings of this study. *[Article copies available for a fee from The Haworth Document Delivery Service: 1-800-HAWORTH. E-mail address: <docdelivery@haworthpress.com> Website: <http://www.HaworthPress.com> © 2003 by The Haworth Press, Inc. All rights reserved.]*

KEYWORDS. Capital structure, trade off theory, pecking order theory, panel data, Mauritius

INTRODUCTION

This paper reviews the capital structure debate and aims to empirically study the determinants of capital structure of non-financial firms quoted on the stock exchange market of Mauritius. Consistent with Rajan and Zingales (1995) the motivation is to assess whether, or which, of the various capital structure theories can stand the test of different markets. If this is the case then firm characteristics that have been found important in determining the capital structure of US firms should be similarly correlated with the leverage ratios of Mauritian firms. However, where the nature of correlation between leverage and other firm characteristics in Mauritius differs from the pattern recorded for US data, this does not necessarily imply a rejection of the underlying theory. Indeed, such deviation could still support theory to the extent that it may be explained by differences in the institutional structure of the Mauritian market.

Capital structure theories are concerned with explaining how the mix of debt and equity in the firm's capital structure influences its market value. Since Modigliani and Miller's (1958) Proposition I, the debate has focused on how capital structure influences the value of the firm when their assumptions are relaxed. Particular attention has been paid to how taxation, financial distress costs, information asymmetries, and agency costs influence the relationship between capital structure and firm value.

The trade off theory introduces into the capital structure debate the benefit of the debt tax shield on the one hand and the cost associated with financial distress on the other. The implication of this theory is that each firm has an optimal debt ratio that maximises value, although this level may vary between firms. Moreover, the trade off theory is often further extended to incorporate agency considerations. This is in the spirit of Jensen and Meckling (1976) who note that debt is valuable in reducing the agency costs of equity but at the same time debt is costly as it increases the agency costs of debt.

Information asymmetries between managers and outside shareholders introduce further complications to the capital structure debate. When managers know that the value of the firm is above its current market value, they will be reluctant to issue equity. Under such circumstances outsiders rely on managers' actions as signals regarding the true value of the firm, and an issue of equity is likely to be interpreted as a bad signal. Thus, to avoid sending bad signals managers will rely primarily on internal funds. When these are insufficient, managers will prefer debt to equity because debt is less sensitive to information asymmetries. This results in what Myers (1984) terms the pecking order theory.

Thus, there is a sharp conflict between the trade off theory, which predicts an optimal capital mix and the pecking order theory, which predicts a financing order. Hence, to distinguish between these competing views, researchers often examine the nature of the correlation between leverage and many other firm characteristics. However, this approach is not always fruitful as the direction of correlation between leverage and a particular firm characteristic can often be explained by more than one theory. Bearing this limitation in mind, the study progresses as follows. Section 2 gives a brief description of the Mauritian economy and corporate sector as a background to the empirical sections that come next. Section 3 presents the model and the theoretical predictions while Section 4 describes the database. Empirical procedures are described in Section 5, estimation and results are given in Section 6, and Section 7 concludes.

THE MAURITIAN ECONOMY AND CORPORATE SECTOR

Dating back to the period of the French colonisation, the Mauritian economy has been based on sugar cultivation and milling. Indeed, this is an important feature that has traditionally characterised the country's economy. However, following the high world sugar price in the 1970s, much of the profits of the sugar sector were invested in sectors other than agriculture. Thus, following a successful diversification of its economic activities away from sugar, the economy rests besides agriculture on three other sectors, namely manufacturing, tourism and financial services.

Another important feature that has traditionally characterised the Mauritian economy is its fairly concentrated ownership structure, with a predominance of family owned groups. Indeed, private ownership of companies and the importance placed on preventing dilution in control is widespread. For example, out of a total of 616 public companies at 31st December 1997, only 46 are on the official list (Registrar of Companies). However, many of these 616 public companies are subsidiaries of companies listed on the Stock Exchange of Mauritius (SEM).

SEM was set up by the Stock Exchange Act of 1988, and it operates two markets. These are the Official Market on which are traded the securities of listed companies, and the over-the-counter (OTC) market for trading securities of unlisted companies. The Official Market began its operations with five listed companies, a market capitalisation of Rs1.4 billion and turnover of Rs14.3 million. However, by 1999 the Mauritian stock market has expanded to list over forty domestic companies, two foreign companies and some sixteen debentures. Table 1 gives the main indicators of the SEM for the period 1989 to 1999.

Though there has been an increase in the number of individual investors on the market from around 6,000 in 1991 to 30,000 at the end of 1996, the latter figure still represents only about 5% of the total population. Indeed, despite good corporate results, local investors tend to shy away from the market. Both the individual and institutional investors tend to cling to their holdings, leading to undue upward pressure on prices under booming market conditions as well as lack of demand for undervalued stocks leading to undue downward pressure on prices during bearish periods. Analysis of the market turnover ratio of the SEM for the past ten years shows that this is between 1% and 5% for most companies, with an average of around only 2.2%. Such a situation of low liquidity leads to high price volatility and renders entry and exit conditions difficult and therefore impacts the informational efficiency of the market in a negative manner.

Thus the Mauritius Stock market is far from the typical capital market. Indeed, the SEM, by virtue of the size of the economy and the restricted business landscape, does not display the breadth and depth of sophisticated stock markets. Further, unlike in developed countries where the stock markets are perceived to broadly replicate the economy, this is not the case in Mauritius. None of the garments manufacturers, which are the largest export earner and a key GDP contributor, is listed on the market. There is a relatively high degree of market concentration, reflecting the special feature of the Mauritian business, which is dominated by a few large companies and conglomerates. For instance, the top ten listed companies on the Exchange account for seventy per-

TABLE 1. Main Indicators of the Stock Exchange of Mauritius

#	1989	1990	1991	1992	1993	1994	1995	1996	1997	1998	1999
No of listed Co Equity	6	13	19	21	29	34	39	42	42	42	43
No of listed Cos (including debentures)	6	14	20	22	30	35	41	45	46	47	48
Market Capitalisation (Rs Million)	1437.1	3792.7	4862.5	6598.9	1490.7	2853.6	2781.7	3337.7	3693.5	4533.5	4173.1
SEMDEX	117	171	154	183	302	474	344	353	391	466	435
Change in SEMDEX	-	45.9	−9.9	18.8	65.2	56.5	−27.2	2.6	10.6	19	−6.4
Traded Value (Rs'million)	14.2	88.5	81.2	158.6	691.6	1555.5	1232.6	1601.7	2997	2556.1	1978.1
Traded Volume p.a (shares)	0.6	3.6	4.5	8.7	37.3	52.5	60.7	92	164.1	98.9	85.3
Trading Sessions	26	51	50	99	97	147	149	148	160	248	250
Average Turnover per session (Rs'million)	0.5	1.7	1.6	1.6	7.1	10.6	8.3	10.8	18.7	10.3	7.9
Weekly Frequency	1	1	1	2	2	2:03	3	3	3:5 *	5	5
P/E Ratio	7.4	8	7	11.6	12	16.5	11.12	14.46	14.06	11.58	8.46
Dividend Yield - %	7.2	6.2	6.1	6	4.2	3.32	5.14	3.97	4.3	4.03	5.54
No of Stockbrokers	27	27	27	27	30	30	31	37	38	39	27
US Dollar Rate	15.41	14.89	15.71	15.58	17.7	18.08	17.8	19.71	21.05	24.51	25.39
Annual Turnover in US$ million	0.92	5.95	5.17	10.18	39.07	86.03	69.25	81.26	142.37	104.3	77.9
Ave Turnover per session US $ million	0.035	0.117	0.103	0.103	0.403	0.585	0.464	0.549	0.89	0.421	0.311
Market Cap in US $ million	93.3	254.7	309.5	423.5	842.2	1578.3	1562.8	1693.4	1754.6	1849.9	1643.3

As at end of period
* Trading sessions were held thrice weekly until 24th November when daily trading started
The 1997 figures include transaction between SMB and Nedbank :: 76.88 ML shares traded for Rs961 ML
Source: Constructed from different sources

cent of the total market capitalisation. Likewise, the top five represents sixty one percent of market capitalisation.

To summarise, there is a firm belief that after ten years of existence, the stock market has had a positive impact on increased savings and investment, on the creation of shareholders' wealth and on overall economic growth. However, the market still suffers from the absence of a strong domestic investor base, over concentration of stock market activities on equities, low level of liquidity and lower standard of disclosure of corporate information than the better-regulated markets. It will be many years before the stock exchange in Mauritius, like those in other developing countries, becomes efficient and more than of minor importance in the capital allocation process. Nevertheless, it is companies on that stock exchange that constitute the database for the empirical procedure, which is discussed next.

A THEORETICAL MODEL OF THE DETERMINANTS OF CAPITAL STRUCTURE

The Model

Based on the capital structure theories discussed in the introduction, and on the basis of previous empirical studies as reviewed in Prasad et al. (2001), it is useful to specify a generic model of capital structure as follows:

$$(LEVERAGE)_{i,t} = \alpha + \beta_1 (AGEINCOR)_{i,t} + \beta_2 (SIZE)_{i,t} + \beta_3 (AVPROFIT)_{i,t} + \beta_4 (GROWTH)_{i,t} + \beta_5 (RISK)_{i,t} + \beta_6 (ASSETS)_{i,t} + \beta_7 (TXSHIELD)_{i,t} + \mu_{i,t} \tag{1}$$

where LEVERAGE is the ratio of short term plus long term liabilities to total assets; AGEINCOR is the number of years since the year of incorporation; SIZE is the natural log of turnover; AVPROFIT is a measure of profitability and is the average ratio of profit before interest and exceptional items to total assets for a period of three years; GROWTH is the annual percentage increase in total assets during the two years up to the current year; RISK is the volatility of earnings which is represented by stock price volatility. A measure of stock price volatility is based on the residuals obtained from a regression of the natural log of the daily stock price on a constant and time; ASSETS is the asset structure, given by the ratio of fixed assets to total assets; TXSHIELD is a proxy for non-debt tax shield measured as the ratio of depreciation to total assets;

A more detailed description of all the variables in Equation (1) is contained in the Appendix, Table A1.

Theoretical Predictions

Given the special case of Mauritius, it is assumed that the pecking order theory should be the more appropriate theory in explaining the capital structure decisions of firms operating in this economy. Specifically, the pecking order theory is predicted to fit the Mauritian case because it is an emerging economy. Indeed, as an emerging economy, and based on the problems characterising the capital market as reviewed in Section 2, the finance gap and information asymmetries which Mauritian companies face are expected to be particularly severe. Thus the hypothesised directions of influence of the explanatory variables on the leverage variable under each of the competing theories is given below, and the expectation is that the empirical findings should be consistent with the direction implied by the pecking order theory.

Age

Based on trade off considerations, it may be argued that as the firm matures, its debt capacity increases implying a positive impact on leverage. However, it may also be argued that as the firm matures it builds reputation leading to better access to equity markets. The latter view implies that age should be negatively related to leverage, and is consistent with pecking order theory. Thus in the case of age the sign on the estimated coefficient distinguishes between the trade off theory, when the sign is expected to be positive, and pecking order considerations, when a negative sign is expected.

Size

A trade off based argument for a positive relationship between size and leverage, is that as the firm grows bigger it becomes more diversified, less risky, and thus less prone to bankruptcy. Larger firms, therefore, have higher debt capacity and a positive link is expected between size and leverage if the trade off theory is valid.

Profitability

In the context of the pecking order theory, profitable firms are likely to have sufficient internal finance that ensures they do not need to rely on external sources. Moreover, in an agency theory framework, if the market for corporate control is inefficient, managers of profitable firms will use the higher levels of retained earnings in order to avoid the disciplinary role of external finance. These two explanations suggest a negative relationship between profitability and leverage. However, it is also possible that as its profitability increases, the firm becomes the target of lenders, who tend to prefer borrowers with high current cash flows. Moreover, in an agency theory framework, if the market for corporate control is efficient, managers of profitable firms will seek debt because they regard it as a commitment to pay out cash in the future as in the context of Jensen (1986). These two explanations support a positive sign on the estimated coefficient of the firm profitability variable.

Growth (Investment Opportunities)

In line with agency theory of debt, conflicts between owners and lenders should lead to a negative relationship between growth and debt levels. These conflicts include two of the agency costs of debt, namely under investment and risk shifting. Considerations based on the trade off theory also point to negative correlation between growth and leverage. For example, although growth opportunities add value, the firm cannot use growth opportunities as security for lenders (Titman and Wessels, 1988). However, in line with pecking order theory growing firms, that need funds, prefer debt to external equity. Thus based on pecking order considerations, the relationship between growth opportunities and leverage is predicted to be positive.

Earnings Volatility (Risk)

Risk is negatively associated with leverage due to trade off considerations. Particularly, the probability of being unable to meet financial obligations increases with the volatility of earnings. As the present value of the costs of financial distress increases with the probability of being financially distress, risky firms prefer less debt. Further, the agency theory of debt also predicts a negative association between debt and risk. Particularly, risk increases the probability of expropriation of debt holders' wealth through risk shifting or under investment, as equity holders are aware that there may be insufficient funds to pay them. Hence, risky firms will use less debt, and there should be a negative association between debt and risk.

Asset Structure

The ratio of fixed to total assets represents the degree of assets' tangibility, which the trade off theory predicts to be positively related to debt levels. Particularly, tangible assets often reduce the costs of financial distress because they tend to have higher liquidation value. For this reason tangible assets normally provide high collateral value relative to intangible assets, which implies that these assets can support more debt. Further, Viswanath and Frierman (1995) note that it is usually more difficult to alter the variance of the cash flows generated from tangible rather than intangible assets. Thus asset tangibility reduces the scope for risk shifting and, consistent with agency theory, firms with tangible assets will support more debt. However, Titman and Wessels (1988) provide an agency theory based argument for a negative relationship between the tangibility of the firm's assets and leverage. Accordingly it is easier to monitor the use of tangible rather than intangible assets, which means that firms with intangible assets will tend to use more debt for monitoring purposes.

Non-Debt Tax Shield

In the context of the trade off theory, non-debt tax shields provide alternative to interest tax shield. Therefore firms with high non-debt tax shields, such as accelerated depreciation and investment tax credits, relative to their expected cash flows, should use less debt. Thus the trade off theory predicts the variable measuring non-debt tax shield to have a negative impact on leverage.

THE DATABASE

This study utilises accounting data and daily stock prices for all non-financial firms listed on the official market in Mauritius for the period 1990 to 2000. However, in spite of having data for eleven years, the empirical analysis covers only the nine years from 1992 to 2000. The reason for the loss of the two earliest years (1990 and 1991) is due to the way some of the variables in the model are defined. In particular, as detailed in the Appendix, Table A1, the variable GROWTH and the variable AVPROFIT are based on data for the current and previous two years.

There are twenty-four non-financial companies on the official market, distributed across five industry sectors as follows. Seven firms are classified under Commerce while a further seven are classified under Industry. Four firms are in Leisure and Hotels, five are in the traditional Sugar business and one is in Transport.[1] The number of years per firm with all the required price and accounting data ranges from four to nine years. Thus the number of available firm/year observations is 165. However, one firm/year observation is dropped due to change in year ending date, leaving a sample size of 164.

Companies' names, their age, average leverage and other variables averaged over the period studied are presented in Table A2 of the Appendix. Table A2 confirms the previously mentioned deep roots of the Mauritian economy in the sugar industry. Indeed, the table shows that listed firms in the sugar industry have, in general, been incorporated much earlier compared with listed firms in other industries. Another interesting observation from Table A2 is the distribution of the average gearing ratios across firms from the same industrial sector. Looking at this distribution, it is not obvious that firms in the same sector have similar capital structures. For example, LEVERAGE in the Commerce sector ranges from just over 20 percent (CMPL) to nearly 70 percent (Rogers & Co). This is in contrast to the observation in Harris and Raviv (1991) where it is noted as a basic stylised fact that firms within an industry tend to have similar capital structures.[2] It is likely, however, that this apparent lack of industry trend in the present sample is due to its small size.[3]

Table 2 presents descriptive statistics of the variables of interest for the 24 firms pooled over the period 1992 to 2000. The correlation matrix of Table 2 does not point to high correlation among the explanatory variables. The highest correlation coefficient (in absolute terms) is that between the proxy for firm profitability, AVPROFIT, and age since incorporation, AGEINCOR, at -0.53. The second highest is the correlation coefficient between the proxy for non-tax shield, TXSHIELD, and AVPROFIT at 0.38. The only other correlation coefficient with an absolute value greater than 0.30 is that between AGEINCOR and TXSHIELD at -0.32.

To assess more directly whether the sample suffers from near multicollinearity, the Variance Inflation Factor (VIF) procedure was applied to the data. The results show that the values for all the VIFs are relatively small, and none of the factors exceeds the value of 2. Consistent with the observation made from studying the correlation matrix of Table 2, the explanatory variables associated with the highest VIF values

TABLE 2. Results of Covariance Procedure for 164 Firm/Year Observations for 24 Non-Financial Firms Listed on the Stock Exchange of Mauritius, 1992-2000

Panel A: Descriptive Statistics

	Mean	Std Dev	Skewness	Kurtosis
LEVERAGE	0.362	0.190	0.291	−0.658
AGEINCOR	42.043	37.844	2.061	4.075
SIZE	20.117	1.175	0.516	−0.013
AVPROFIT	0.094	0.050	0.400	0.347
GROWTH	0.143	0.141	1.853	6.555
RISK	0.060	0.038	1.977	4.921
ASSETS	0.604	0.196	−0.321	−0.429
TXSHIELD	0.037	0.026	1.345	1.363

Panel B: Correlation Matrix

	LEVER-AGE	AGE-INCOR	SIZE	AV-PROFIT	GROWTH	RISK	ASSETS	TX-SHIELD
LEVERAGE	1.000							
AGEINCOR	−0.425	1.000						
SIZE	0.602	−0.202	1.000					
AVPROFIT	0.119	−0.529	−0.008	1.000				
GROWTH	0.062	−0.067	0.206	0.225	1.000			
RISK	0.054	0.063	0.008	−0.072	−0.080	1.000		
ASSETS	−0.455	0.171	−0.247	−0.090	0.122	−0.249	1.000	
TXSHIELD	0.200	−0.319	−0.120	0.381	−0.262	−0.065	−0.060	1.000

include AVPROFIT (1.73), AGEINCOR (1.54) and TXSHIELD (1.42).[4] Thus as the VIFs as well as the descriptive statistics presented in Table 2 appear reasonable, the next stage is the empirical analysis.

EMPIRICAL PROCEDURE

The initial empirical analysis is based on variables as defined in Equation (1). However the analysis is then expanded, by exploring alternative proxies to measure some of the variables of interest. In particular, alternative proxies are used to measure four of the explanatory variables, namely asset structure, non-debt tax shield, firm size and firm age. There are thus sixteen different variations of Equation (1).[5]

For each of the sixteen variants of Equation (1), the PANEL command in TSP 4.4 produces four regressions: the TOTAL model, the FIXED effects model, the BETWEEN model and the RANDOM effects model. The first three models produce Ordinary Least Squares (OLS) estimates while the RANDOM effect model produces Feasible Generalised Least Squares (FGLS) estimates. The FIXED and RANDOM effects models relax the assumption that the intercept coefficients are constant across firms. The FIXED effects model takes α_i to be firm-specific constant terms while the RANDOM effects model takes α_i to be firm-specific disturbance terms that are constant across time for each firm.

Various tests are also produced to assist in selecting the most appropriate model. For example, to assist in deciding between the TOTAL and FIXED effect model, TSP 4.4 prints the results of an F-test for the significance of the firm-specific effects, where the null hypothesis is that there are no firm-specific effects: $\alpha_1 = \alpha_2 = \ldots = \alpha_{n-1} = 0$. Providing the FIXED effects model is preferred to the TOTAL specification, the question is whether the RANDOM model should be preferred to the FIXED effects model. For this purpose, the TSP 4.4 PANEL command generates the Hausman's Test for fixed verses random effects. Under the FIXED effects specifications there is no need to assume that the firm specific effects, α_i, are uncorrelated with the other regressors. However, under the RANDOM effects specifications the specific effects are random and part of the disturbance terms. Under such specifications, if the firm specific effects are correlated with any of the explanatory variables, this would lead to the omitted variable problem resulting in the estimated coefficients becoming inconsistent.

The Hausman Test utilises this difference to test for the RANDOM effects model verses the FIXED effects model. In particular the null hypothesis is of no correlation between the random firm-specific effects and any of the explanatory variables. In this case both the OLS estimates from the FIXED effects regression and the FGLS estimates from the RANDOM effects regression are consistent but the former are inefficient due to autocorrelation in the disturbance terms. Under the alternative hypothesis the OLS estimates from the FIXED effects regression are consistent but the FGLS estimates from the RANDOM effects regression are inconsistent due to correlation between the disturbance terms and the explanatory variables.

Based on this observation and on the idea that the covariance of an efficient estimator with its difference from an inefficient estimator is zero, the Hausman Test can be derived as shown in Greene (1997, pp. 632-633). Rejection of the test statistic is a rejection of the null hypothesis that the coefficient estimates from the RANDOM effects model are consistent, leading to preference for the FIXED effects model over the RANDOM effects model.

ESTIMATION AND TESTING RESULTS

The results for the sixteen variations of Equation (1) are given in Table 3. Table 3 reports only the results from the RANDOM effects specification. Indeed, as indicated, the Hausman Test statistic for all but one specification (Model 15) does not reject the null hypothesis. The results across the sixteen specifications are generally consistent and tell an interesting story.

The estimated coefficient on age since incorporation, AGEINCOR, enters with a negative sign in the eight specifications in which it is included (Model 1-Model 8). Furthermore, it is consistently significant at the 1 percent significance level. Similarly, the estimated coefficient on age since listing on the SEM, AGELIST, enters with a negatively signed estimated coefficient, in seven out of eight models in which it is included (It is positively signed in Model 16). However, unlike age since incorporation, age since listing on the SEM is never significant. As discussed in Sub-section 3.2, the impact of age on leverage is consistent with pecking order considerations but not with the trade off theory. Further, the relative importance of age since incorporation, as opposed age since listing on the SEM, may be explained in terms of the recent origin of the SEM and may point to the unimportant role it plays as a source of capital for firms.

Strong and positive relationship emerges from the empirical analysis between firm size and leverage. Whether size is measured as the log of turnover (SIZE) or as the log of total assets (SIZE2), the estimated coefficients under all specifications are consistently positive and significant at the 1 percent level. These findings are inconsistent with Titman and Wessels (1988), but are in line with the general findings in Alderson and Betker (1995), Rajan and Zingales (1995), Wiwattanakantang (1999), Jordan et al. (1998), Hussain (1997) and Hirota (1999), amongst others. Furthermore, the results for the size variable are the only findings of this study, which offer strong support for the trade off theory.

The estimated coefficient on the firm profitability measure, AVPROFIT, is negatively signed across the sixteen specifications and is also significant at the 5 percent level or more in all models but Model 16. A negative association between profitability and leverage is inconsistent with the trade off theory but is in line with the pecking order theory and with

TABLE 3. Results of Panel Procedure: RANDOM Effects for 164 Firm/Year Observations for 24 Non-Financial Firms Listed on the Stock Exchange of Mauritius, 1992-2000

Panel A: Models 1-4 with AGEINCOR and SIZE, and with alternative measures for asset structure and for non-debt tax shield

Dependent: LEVERAGE												
Model:	1			2			3			4		
F test of A B = Ai B: F(23 133)	22.663	[.0000]		23.798	[.0000]		26.265	[.0000]		26.990	[.0000]	
THETA	0.034			0.032			0.029			0.028		
Adjusted R-squared	0.526			0.488			0.507			0.474		
LM het. Test	0.021	[.884]		2.082	[.149]		1.166	[.280]		5.022	[.025]	
Std. Error of regression	0.131			0.136			0.134			0.138		
Hausman test CHISQ(7)	4.362	[.7373]		5.631	[.5834]		3.399	[.8458]		3.194	[.8665]	
Variable	Co-efficient	t-statistic	P-value	Co-efficient	t-statistic	P-value	Co-efficient	t-statistic	P-value	Co-efficient	t-statistic	P-value
AGEINCOR	-0.002	-3.048	[.002]	-0.002	-3.135	[.002]	-0.002	-3.117	[.002]	-0.002	-3.179	[.001]
SIZE	0.059	4.306	[.000]	0.062	4.264	[.000]	0.066	4.706	[.000]	0.069	4.720	[.000]
AVPROFIT	-0.917	-4.250	[.000]	-0.913	-4.080	[.000]	-0.683	-3.029	[.002]	-0.659	-2.815	[.005]
GROWTH	0.130	2.946	[.003]	0.122	2.674	[.008]	0.107	2.528	[.011]	0.097	2.208	[.027]
RISK	0.066	0.472	[.637]	0.092	0.646	[.518]	0.104	0.763	[.445]	0.132	0.943	[.345]
ASSETS	-0.285	-4.112	[.000]				-0.267	-3.875	[.000]			
TANGIBLE				-0.206	-2.721	[.006]				-0.185	-2.472	[.013]
TXSHIELD	0.679	1.180	[.238]	0.734	1.241	[.215]						
TAX							0.248	2.969	[.003]	0.261	3.051	[.002]
C	-0.529	-1.762	[.078]	-0.597	-1.848	[.065]	-0.874	-2.693	[.007]	-0.976	-2.815	[.005]

Panel B: Models 5-8 with AGEINCOR and SIZE2, and with alternative measures for asset structure and for non-debt tax shield

Dependent: LEVERAGE												
Model:	5			6			7			8		
F test of A B = Ai B: F(23 133)	23.176	[.0000]		24.632	[.0000]		28.026	[.0000]		28.693	[.0000]	
THETA	0.033			0.031			0.027			0.026		
Adjusted R-squared	0.539			0.482			0.467			0.414		
LM het. test	0.248	[.618]		2.021	[.155]		0.105	[.746]		1.994	[.158]	
Std. error of regression	0.129			0.137			0.140			0.146		
Hausman test CHISQ(7)	6.737	[.4568]		6.897	[.4397]		5.766	[.5673]		6.950	[.4342]	
Variable	Co-efficient	t-statistic	P-value	Co-efficient	t-statistic	P-value	Co-efficient	t-statistic	P-value	Co-efficient	t-statistic	P-value
AGEINCOR	−0.003	−4.045	[.000]	−0.003	−4.025	[.000]	−0.003	−4.036	[.000]	−0.003	−4.075	[.000]
SIZE2	0.073	5.150	[.000]	0.076	4.905	[.000]	0.064	4.508	[.000]	0.065	4.315	[.000]
AVPROFIT	−0.727	−3.328	[.001]	−0.703	−3.044	[.002]	−0.584	−2.516	[.012]	−0.554	−2.276	[.023]
GROWTH	0.104	2.353	[.019]	0.092	1.996	[.046]	0.085	1.930	[.054]	0.074	1.600	[.110]
RISK	0.077	0.561	[.574]	0.106	0.757	[.449]	0.101	0.743	[.457]	0.131	0.933	[.351]
ASSETS	−0.276	−4.084	[.000]				−0.280	−4.084	[.000]			
TANGIBLE				−0.173	−2.290	[.022]				−0.182	−2.401	[.016]
TXSHIELD	1.723	2.894	[.004]	1.791	2.903	[.004]						
TAX							0.212	2.561	[.010]	0.222	2.612	[.009]
C	−0.871	−2.739	[.006]	−0.960	−2.705	[.007]	−0.791	−2.475	[.013]	−0.867	−2.465	[.014]

TABLE 3 (continued)

Panel C: Models 9-12 with AGELIST and SIZE, and with alternative measures for asset structure and for non-debt tax shield

Dependent: LEVERAGE												
Model:	9			10			11			12		
F test of A B = Ai B: F(23.133)	24.670 [.0000]			27.738 [.0000]			29.103 [.0000]			31.403 [.0000]		
THETA	0.031			0.027			0.026			0.024		
Adjusted R-squared	0.429			0.341			0.373			0.300		
LM het. test	5.650 [.017]			6.718 [.010]			13.510 [.000]			14.821 [.000]		
Std. error of re-gression	0.145			0.156			0.151			0.159		
Hausman test CHISQ(7)	14.471 [.0434]			13.796 [.0549]			14.754 [.0393]			12.581 [.0830]		
Variable	Co-efficient	t-statistic	P-value	Co-efficient	t-statistic	P-value	Co-efficient	t-statistic	P-value	Co-efficient	t-statistic	P-value
AGELIST	−0.002	−0.608	[.543]	0.000	−0.090	[.929]	−0.002	−0.760	[.447]	−0.001	−0.268	[.788]
SIZE	0.065	4.058	[.000]	0.064	3.812	[.000]	0.073	4.381	[.000]	0.073	4.224	[.000]
AVPROFIT	−0.788	−3.472	[.001]	−0.718	−3.008	[.003]	−0.561	−2.414	[.016]	−0.480	−1.975	[.048]
GROWTH	0.130	2.924	[.003]	0.117	2.569	[.010]	0.101	2.386	[.017]	0.088	2.017	[.044]
RISK	0.061	0.431	[.666]	0.103	0.713	[.476]	0.101	0.734	[.463]	0.143	1.011	[.312]
ASSETS	−0.287	−3.853	[.000]				−0.272	−3.669	[.000]			
TANGIBLE				−0.166	−2.002	[.045]				−0.151	−1.848	[.065]
TXSHIELD	0.949	1.645	[.100]	0.936	1.556	[.120]						
TAX							0.260	3.076	[.002]	0.268	3.096	[.002]
C	−0.733	−2.268	[.023]	−0.792	−2.303	[.021]	−1.105	−3.101	[.002]	−1.198	−3.196	[.001]

144

Panel D: Models 13-16 with AGELIST and SIZE2, and with alternative measures for asset structure and for non-debt tax shield

Dependent: LEVERAGE												
Model:	13			14			15			16		
F test of A B = Ai B: F(23 133)	29.369	[.0000]		34.228	[.0000]		35.694	[.0000]		38.765	[.0000]	
THETA	0.026			0.022			0.021			0.020		
Adjusted R-squared	0.347			0.221			0.200			0.097		
LM het. test	6.034	[.014]		3.507	[.061]		1.549	[.213]		0.066	[.797]	
Std. error of regression	0.154			0.168			0.172			0.183		
Hausman test CHISQ(7)	18.453	[.0101]		15.618	[.0288]		19.928	[.0057]		17.939	[.0122]	
Variable	Co-efficient	t-statistic	P-value	Co-efficient	t-statistic	P-value	Co-efficient	t-statistic	P-value	Co-efficient	t-statistic	P-value
AGELIST	−0.005	−1.372	[.170]	−0.002	−0.608	[.543]	−0.001	−0.444	[.657]	0.001	0.246	[.806]
SIZE2	0.080	4.199	[.000]	0.076	3.647	[.000]	0.057	3.122	[.002]	0.053	2.747	[.006]
AVPROFIT	−0.641	−2.843	[.004]	−0.553	−2.304	[.021]	−0.466	−1.965	[.049]	−0.374	−1.492	[.136]
GROWTH	0.105	2.345	[.019]	0.093	1.974	[.048]	0.093	2.063	[.039]	0.083	1.748	[.080]
RISK	0.053	0.385	[.700]	0.103	0.724	[.469]	0.098	0.709	[.478]	0.144	1.018	[.309]
ASSETS	−0.301	−4.052	[.000]				−0.283	−3.741	[.000]			
TANGIBLE				−0.152	−1.818	[.069]				−0.138	−1.655	[.098]
TXSHIELD	2.109	3.244	[.001]	1.967	2.880	[.004]						
TAX							0.210	2.513	[.012]	0.212	2.469	[.014]
C	−1.105	−2.770	[.006]	−1.106	−2.507	[.012]	−0.768	−2.001	[.045]	−0.785	−1.896	[.058]

agency theory when the market for corporate control is inefficient. Indeed it appears that Mauritian firms, which are typically associated with particular families, do not like the restrictions or the disclosure of information that come with debt. Thus when profits are sufficient to meet their financing needs, leverage tends to be lower. Other studies including Titman and Wessels (1988), Rajan and Zingales (1995), Wiwattanakantang (1999), and Hirota (1999) generally find profitability to be negatively related to leverage. However, it is not uncommon to find differing empirical results in the literature. For example, in Hussain (1997) the estimated coefficient on the profitability measure is positive and significant in the case of Korea, but negative and significant in the case of Malaysia. Likewise Jordan et al. (1998) find the sign on the estimated coefficients on the profitability variable to be consistently positive, although insignificantly so in the FGLS regression.

The measure of growth in total assets, GROWTH, appears with a positive estimated coefficient across all specifications. GROWTH is also significant at the 10 percent level at least, in all models apart of Model 8. A positive link between firm growth and leverage is consistent with pecking order theory but inconsistent with the trade off and agency theories. Furthermore, previous studies have, on the main, reported negative association between growth and leverage. For example, negative but insignificant relationship between growth and leverage is reported in Titman and Wessels (1988) and in Jordan et al. (1998). Similarly, Rajan and Zingales (1995), Wiwattanakantang (1999), and Hirota (1999) report negative and significant impact of growth on leverage. However, in the Mauritian context, a positive association between firm growth and leverage could be rationalised as follows. Mauritian firms basically rely on bank loans and retained earnings. Indeed this is reflected in the small number of corporate debentures traded on the Mauritian capital market and in the relatively thin trading that takes place on the SEM as discussed in Section 2. Thus as the choice is essentially between loans and retained earnings, growing firms with little of the latter have no choice but to seek debt finance. This could explain the positive association between GROWTH and the dependent variable.

The proxy that is meant to measure earnings volatility and firm risk is the variable RISK, which is measured in terms of stock price volatility. The estimated coefficient on RISK is consistently positive and insignificant across all specifications. These findings are inconsistent with the prediction of a negative impact of risk on leverage based on the trade off and agency theories. However, failure to find strong evidence for the importance of risk in the firm leverage decision is also reflected in the results of other studies. Specifically, Bradley et al. (1984) show the estimated coefficient on the firm risk variable to be negative and significant while Jordan et al. (1998) show it to be significant but positive. In Titman and Wessels (1988), Wiwattanakantang (1999) and Hirota (1999) evidence concerning risk is generally weak. Moreover, in the context of Mauritius it could be argued that stock price volatility does not reflect earnings volatility, because of the inactive nature of the SEM.

The results are relatively strong for the asset structure of the firm, whether it is measured by the ratio of fixed to total assets, ASSETS, or by the ratio of fixed assets plus inventories to total assets, TANGIBLE. The estimated coefficients on both proxies are consistently negatively signed and significant, although the first measure (ASSETS) shows stronger results as it is consistently significant at the 1 percent level. This negative association between tangibility and debt is inconsistent with the trade off based explanations given in Sub-section 3.2. It is also inconsistent with the agency rationale according to which leverage will be higher for firms with many tangible assets because it is more difficult to engage in risk shifting when tangible assets are already in place. Furthermore, these findings are inconsistent with the results in Rajan and Zingales (1995), Wiwattanakantang (1999), Jordan et al. (1998) and Hirota (1999). However, a negative relationship between asset structure and leverage, is consistent with the agency-based rationale concerning the monitoring role of debt. Furthermore, many fixed assets may imply high operating leverage, which leads firms to seek lower financial leverage. This explanation fits particularly well with the observation that when tangibility is measured in terms of fixed assets alone (ASSETS) it appears more significant compared to when it is measured in terms of fixed assets plus inventories (TANGIBLE).

The non-debt tax shield is measured alternatively by the ratio of depreciation to total assets (TXSHIELD) and by the ratio of total expenses less interest to turnover (TAX). Both proxies are included as measures of the availability of non-debt tax shields. However, while depreciation relates to investment in capital assets as a means to reduce tax burden, expenses relate to operation of the company. Since the subject of this paper is capital structure, there is possibly greater justification for using the original proxy, namely TXSHIELD. Nonetheless, irrespective of whether TXSHIELD or TAX is included, the estimated coefficient is consistently positively signed. In the case of TAX it is also consistently significant at least at the 5 percent level, while in the case of TXSHIELD it is significant in five out of eight models in which it is included. A positive association between non-debt tax shields and the use of leverage is contrary to the trade off based prediction as discussed in Sub-section 3.2. It is also at odds with the negative and significant association between non-debt tax shields and leverage as arising from the general results in Wiwattanakantang (1999) and Hirota (1999). In contrast Alderson and Betker (1995) and Titman and Wessels (1988) show weak results with regards the association between the non-debt tax shield and leverage. Still, although the rationale for a positive relationship between alternative tax shield and the use of debt is puzzling, it is not uncommon in the literature. For example Bradley et al. (1984) also report a positive and significant association between the non-debt tax shield and leverage.

Lastly, the intercept, C, is consistently negatively signed and significant at the 10 percent level or more. Although no prediction was made regarding the sign on the intercept, a negative sign is consistent with the results in Hussain (1997).[6] It is inconsistent, however, with other empirical results including Bradley et al. (1984), Alderson and Betker (1995), and Jordan et al. (1998). As the constant, C, is the last variable in Table 3 to be discussed, attention is now turned to the concluding remarks.

CONCLUSIONS

In general the results from the panel data procedure seem to support the pecking order theory and reject the trade off theory of capital structure. Indeed the signs of the variables age, profitability, growth, asset structure, non-debt tax shield and risk contradicts the trade off based predictions. (Although the variable risk does not appear important in explaining the leverage decision of non-financial Mauritian listed firms.) At the same time the results with respect age, profitability, and growth support the pecking order theory. In contrast, firm size provides strong evidence in support of the trade off theory. Thus, unless the positive sign between size and leverage can be explained by other theories, such as agency theory, than this inconsistency clearly calls for further investigation.

However, the Mauritian set up also offers a unique opportunity to testing capital structure theories. This is because the market for publicly traded corporate debt is limited thus the financing choice is basically between internal funds, private loans and external equity. Further, due to three features of the Mauritian market, the choice of finance for Mauritian firms is practically between internal funds and private loans.

These three features include the family ownership orientation of the typical Mauritian business, the apparent inefficiency of the market for corporate control, and the development stage of the capital market for equity. Indeed the empirical results reflect these three features of the Mauritian business environment as summarised below.

First, the importance of maintaining control with existing owners is reflected in the negative association between profitability and debt and the positive association between growth and debt. Specifically, firms with insufficient retained earnings prefer external debt to external equity because the former does not involve giving up control. For the same reason growing firms with greater needs for external funds rely more heavily on external debt.

Second, the inefficiency of the market for corporate control is also reflected in the nature of the association between debt and both profitability and growth. Particularly, the negative association between profitability and debt implies that when they have the opportunity to do so, managers prefer to avoid the discipline associated with external funds. Likewise it could be argued that had the market for corporate control been efficient, a negative relationship should have emerged between debt and growth as growing firms would have preferred external equity to external debt.

Third, the small part played by the equity market as a source of funds for Mauritius firms is reflected in the importance of age since incorporation relative to age since listing on the SEM. Similar conclusions emerge from the inadequacy of stock price volatility to reflect firm risk.

Thus the empirical results highlight three distinctive features of the Mauritian business environment and could therefore be of particular value to policy makers. For example the apparent narrow choice over sources of finance for corporate investment should be of concern to policy makers as expansion of these sources may contribute to economic growth. Second, there is also indication that the impact of setting up a capital market in an emerging country like Mauritius may have insignificant impact on the capital structure decisions of firms, at least in the short term. Thus, policies other than those concerned with developing the capital market may need to be considered if firms are to be encouraged to optimise their capital structure.

Finally the results with respect to asset structure and the availability of non-debt tax shields are inconsistent with both the theoretical prediction and previous work. A possible explanation for the negative impact of asset tangibility on leverage could be operational leverage, which heavy investment in fixed assets reflects. However, the positive impact of the availability of alternative tax shields is puzzling. Clearly more research is required to explore these inconsistencies which may be due in part to inadequate selection of proxies.

NOTES

1. In addition to the five non-financial sectors, there are another two financial sectors on the official market, which were excluded from this study. These are the Banks and Insurance sector and the Investments sector.

2. The observation in Harris and Raviv (1991) is consistent with a number of empirical studies. For example, Bradley, Jarrell and Kim (1984), conclude that debt ratios are strongly related to industry classification even when regulated firms are excluded. Titman and Wessels (1988) suggest that the type of assets firms hold is influenced by their industry and for that reason industry classification should also influence debt levels. Hussain (1997) suggests that some industries may enjoy better access to loans due to government policy.

3. The apparent lack of trend in the debt ratios of the sample firms across industries, is puzzling and may be an indication that by excluding non-quoted firms, the sample is not a good reflection of the Mauritian corporate sector as a whole. The fact that this study does not consider industrial classification is due to the small sample size properties of the data.

4. Results of the VIFs can be obtained from the authors.

5. The definitions for the additional proxies are presented in Table A1 of the Appendix.

6. Hussain (1997) finds the constant to be negative and significant for both Korea and Malaysia in all but two of the total regressions.

REFERENCES

Alderson, M.J. and B.L. Betker, (1995), Liquidation costs and capital structure, *Journal of Financial Economics*, 39 (1), 45-69.

Bradley, M., G.A. Jarrell and E.H. Kim, (1984), On the existence of an optimal capital structure: Theory and evidence, *Journal of Finance*, 39 (3), 857-880.

Greene, W.H., (1997), *Econometric Analysis*, 3rd edition, New Jersey: Prentice-Hall.

Harris, M. and A. Raviv, (1991), The theory of capital structure, *Journal of Finance*, 46 (1), 297-355.

Hirota, S., (1999), Are corporate financing decisions different in Japan? An empirical study on capital structure, *Journal of the Japanese and International Economies*, 13 (3), 201-229.

Hsiao, C., (1999), *Analysis of Panel Data*, Cambridge: Cambridge University Press.

Hussain, Q., (1997), The determinants of capital structure: A panel study of Korea and Malaysia, In Kowalski, T. (ed.), *Financial Reform in Emerging Market Economies: Quantitative and Institutional Issues*, Poznan: Akademia Ekonomiczna w Poznaniu, 209-228.

Jensen, M.C., (1986), Agency costs of free cash flow, corporate finance and takeovers, *American Economic Review*, 76, 323-339.

Jensen, M.C. and W. Meckling, (1976), Theory of the firm: Managerial behaviour, agency costs, and capital structure, *Journal of Financial Economics*, 3, 305-360.

Jordan, J., J. Lowe and P. Taylor, (1998), Strategy and financial policy in UK small firms, *Journal of Business Finance and Accounting*, 25 (1&2), 1-27.

Modigliani, F. and M.H. Miller, (1958), The cost of capital, corporation finance and the theory of investment, *American Economic Review*, 48, 261-297.

Myers, S.C., (1984), The capital structure puzzle, *Journal of Finance*, 39, 575-592.

Prasad, S., C.J. Green and V. Murinde, (2001), Company financing, capital structure, and ownership: A survey, and implications for developing economies, *SUERF Studies No. 12*.

Rajan, R.G. and L. Zingales, (1995), What do we know about capital structure? Some evidence from international data, *The Journal of Finance*, 50 (5), 1421-1460.

Titman, S. and R. Wessels, (1988), The determinants of capital structure choice, *Journal of Finance*, 43 (1), 1-19.

Viswanath, P.V. and M. Frierman, (1995), Asset fungibility and equilibrium capital structure, *Journal of Economics and Business*, 47 (4), 319-334.

Wiwattanakantang, Y., (1999), An empirical study on the determinants of the capital structure of Thai firms, *Pacific-Basin Finance Journal*, 7 (3-4), 371-403.

APPENDIX

TABLE A1
Variable Definitions

Variable	Definition
LEVERAGE	The dependent variable: (Long term liabilities + Short term liabilities)/Total assets
AGEINCOR	Firm age: Number of years since the year of incorporation (YEAR–Year of incorporation)
AGELIST	Firm age: Number of years since the year of listing (YEAR–Year of listing)
SIZE	Firm size: Natural log of turnover
SIZE2	Firm size: Natural log of total assets
AVPROFIT	Firm profitability: Average of [(PROFIT,t),(PROFIT,t-1),(PROFIT,t-2)], where PROFIT for year t is defined as PROFIT,t = Profit Before Interest & Exceptional Items/Total assets
GROWTH	Rate of annual growth in assets over current and past 2 years. Defined as: [(TOTAL ASSETS t)/(TOTAL ASSETS t-2)]$^{1/2}$−1
RISK	Volatility of earnings: The mean of the absolute values of the residuals obtained from yearly regressions for each firm, i, of the form: Natural Log of (Daily adj. Price) on a constant and time. The price regressions were run for each of the 24 firms in each of the 9 years from 1992 to 2000. However, only 192 regressions were run because in 24 firm/year cases no daily price data was available. These 24 cases include: 10 firms in 1992; 7 firms in 1993; 5 firms in 1994; 2 firms in 1995. For the 192 regressions, the number of daily price observations per regression varies from 10 (one firm in 1994) to 250 (all firms in 1999). The average number of observations per regression is 147 and the median is 146. Finally, as the year 2000 was not over when the data was collected, the number of observations for each of the 24 regressions for the year 2000, is 26.
ASSETS	Asset structure: Fixed assets/Total assets
TANGIBLE	Asset structure: (Inventory + Fixed assets)/Total assets
TXSHIELD	Non-debt tax shield: Depreciation/Total assets
TAX	Non-debt tax shield: (Total expenses–Interest)/Turnover

TABLE A2

Means for 24 non-financial firms listed on the Stock Exchange of Mauritius, 1992-2000 (Unbalanced data: minimum time periods per firm = 4 years; maximum time periods per firm = 9 years; total firm/year observations = 164)

Firmid	COMPANY NAME	LEVER-AGE	AGE-INCOR	SIZE	AV-PROFIT	GROWTH	RISK	ASSETS	TX-SHIELD
	Commerce								
1	CMPL	0.215	22.5	18.704	0.030	0.022	0.068	0.822	0.031
2	COURTS (MAURITIUS) LTD	0.430	12.0	20.339	0.125	0.183	0.101	0.167	0.012
3	HAPPY WORLD FOODS LTD	0.392	24.5	20.714	0.116	0.267	0.044	0.542	0.032
4	HAREL MALLAC & CO. LTD	0.407	39.5	20.035	0.105	0.124	0.068	0.358	0.035
5	IRELAND BLYTH LTD	0.570	25.0	21.991	0.062	0.125	0.067	0.391	0.037
6	ROGERS & COMPANY LTD	0.681	47.5	22.643	0.085	0.146	0.092	0.555	0.031
7	SHELL MAURITIUS LTD	0.610	6.0	21.354	0.125	0.057	0.053	0.451	0.051
	Industry								
8	GAMMA-CIVIC LTD	0.621	36.0	20.084	0.098	0.238	0.069	0.484	0.063
9	MAURITIUS BREWERIES LTD	0.187	36.0	20.254	0.133	0.191	0.062	0.724	0.055
10	MCFI (Mauritius Chemical & Fertilizer Industry Ltd)	0.285	20.5	20.070	0.071	0.077	0.042	0.486	0.042
11	MAURITIUS OIL REFINERIES LTD (MOROIL)	0.305	27.0	19.586	0.091	0.139	0.057	0.634	0.038
12	MAURITIUS STATIONERY LTD	0.442	29.5	18.910	0.114	0.109	0.044	0.623	0.043
13	PLASTIC INDUSTRY (MTIUS) LTD	0.576	25.0	17.764	0.119	0.044	0.065	0.469	0.081
14	THE UNITED BASALT PRODUCTS LTD	0.366	42.5	19.952	0.141	0.088	0.060	0.517	0.090
	Leisure & hotels								
15	AUTOMATIC SYSTEMS LTD	0.283	5.5	19.664	0.163	0.053	0.044	0.793	0.110
16	GRAND BAIE HOTEL LTD	0.271	16.0	19.146	0.216	0.299	0.035	0.911	0.019
17	NEW MAURITIUS HOTELS LTD	0.418	33.5	21.029	0.098	0.269	0.037	0.911	0.021
18	SUN RESORTS LTD	0.412	13.0	21.028	0.104	0.228	0.039	0.859	0.018

APPENDIX TABLE A2 (continued)

Firmid	COMPANY NAME	LEVER-AGE	AGE-INCOR	SIZE	AV-PROFIT	GROWTH	RISK	ASSETS	TX-SHIELD
	Sugar								
19	HAREL FRERES LTD	0.290	35.5	20.404	0.049	0.159	0.053	0.780	0.024
20	MON DESERT ALMA LTD	0.187	168.5	19.477	0.006	0.062	0.064	0.741	0.019
21	MON TRESOR & MON DESERT LTD	0.115	69.5	19.811	0.119	0.298	0.056	0.686	0.016
22	SAVANNAH SUGAR ESTATES LTD	0.150	113.0	19.473	0.045	0.101	0.058	0.602	0.017
23	THE MOUNT SUGAR ESTATES LTD	0.070	82.5	18.682	0.040	0.126	0.078	0.693	0.011
	Transport								
24	AIR MAURITIUS LTD	0.705	30.5	22.480	0.060	0.186	0.043	0.467	0.024

Financial Reform and Financing Decisions of Listed Firms in Zimbabwe

Enard Mutenheri
Christopher J. Green

SUMMARY. We examine the impact of the economic reform programme on the financing choices of Zimbabwean listed companies. Using the published accounts of a sample of companies, we show that listed firms rely heavily on external finance, especially short-term bank financing. We estimate an eclectic econometric model of firms' capital structure based on key predictions from the theory of finance, augmented by variables aimed at capturing the impact of Zimbabwe's reform programme. The analysis shows that an orthodox model has little explanatory power over firms' capital structure in the pre-reform period, but in the post-re-

Enard Mutenheri and Christopher J. Green are affiliated with Department of Economics, Loughborough University. (Enard Mutenheri is a doctoral candidate at Loughborough University).

An earlier draft of this paper was presented at the second annual Finance and Development Research Programme conference, "Development and Business Finance: Policy and Experience in Developing Countries," held at the University of Manchester on April 5-6, 2001; and funded by The Department for International Development (DFID). We thank participants in this conference for their useful comments. Mutenheri's doctoral research is funded by NUFU. Green's contribution forms part of a general research programme on finance and development funded by DFID. We thank NUFU and DFID for their financial support.

The interpretations and conclusions expressed in this paper are entirely our own and should not be attributed in any manner to NUFU or to DFID.

[Haworth co-indexing entry note]: "Financial Reform and Financing Decisions of Listed Firms in Zimbabwe." Mutenheri, Enard, and Christopher J. Green. Co-published simultaneously in *Journal of African Business* (International Business Press, an imprint of The Haworth Press, Inc.) Vol. 4, No. 2, 2003, pp. 155-170; and: *African Business Finance and Development Policy* (eds: Victor Murinde and Atsede Woldie) International Business Press, an imprint of The Haworth Press, Inc., 2003, pp. 155-170. Single or multiple copies of this article are available for a fee from The Haworth Document Delivery Service [1-800-HAWORTH, 9:00 a.m. - 5:00 p.m. (EST). E-mail address: docdelivery@haworthpress.com].

form period it does better. The differences between the pre-reform and post-reform era suggest that the reforms achieved partial success in opening up the capital markets and improving the transparency of firm financing behaviour. *[Article copies available for a fee from The Haworth Document Delivery Service: 1-800-HAWORTH. E-mail address: <docdelivery@ haworthpress.com> Website: <http://www.HaworthPress.com> © 2003 by The Haworth Press, Inc. All rights reserved.]*

KEYWORDS. Zimbabwe, corporate finance, financial reform

INTRODUCTION

It is widely agreed that the emergence of a dynamic business sector is an important ingredient in the process of economic development in poorer countries. In this respect, a crucial issue is to understand how firms in developing countries finance their activities and how changes in economic policy impact on these financing decisions. However, as Prasad, Green and Murinde (2001) point out, very little is known about company financing decisions in developing countries. Even the basic facts are by no means agreed. The seminal studies of Singh and Hamid (1992) and Singh (1995) utilized company accounts data covering the largest companies in selected developing countries within the International Finance Corporation (IFC) database. They found that, in comparison with firms in OECD countries, firms in developing countries generally utilize a greater proportion of external funding than internal funding and a greater proportion of equity finance than debt finance. Given that capital markets in developing countries are invariably less well developed than in the industrial countries, especially for equities, these findings were surprising. However, Cobham and Subramaniam (1998) argued that the findings were in part an artefact of Singh and Hamid's methodology and sampling, which they claimed biased the statistics in favour of external funding. Concentrating on a single country (India), but using larger samples of companies and a different methodology based on work by Mayer (1988) and by Corbett and Jenkinson (1997), they argued that external and equity funding ratios in India were substantially lower than claimed by Singh and Hamid. A further study of the accounts of large companies in 10 developing countries using the IFC database by Booth, Aivazian, Demirguc-Kunt and Maksimovic (2001; hereafter: BADM) utilized a methodology proposed by Rajan and Zingales (1995), and found that debt ratios varied substantially across developing countries, but overall were not out of line with comparable data for OECD countries.

A partial reconciliation of the different methodologies employed by previous researchers was discussed by Green, Murinde and Suppakitjarak (2001; hereafter: GMS) who also analysed a large sample of Indian company accounts. Their results broadly confirmed Singh and Hamid's findings on external funding ratios but not on debt ratios which, like BADM, they found to be more in line with OECD data. Crucially however, they found that time-and company-averages could conceal considerable changes in company behaviour. In India, there were measurable, significant changes over time in external funding and debt ratios. Many of these could have been related to the economic reform programmes undertaken in India during the late-1980s and early 1990s, but GMS did not test this hypothesis explicitly. It is clearly reasonable to expect that company financing patterns in developing countries will evolve over time as capital markets develop, and in response to any economic reform programmes which may be undertaken. Therefore an essential next step in understanding company financing in developing economies is to examine how far the data are influenced by economic policy changes in different countries.

In this paper we take up the theme of company financing and economic reform, and empirically examine the impact of economic reform programmes on the financing choices of the corporate sector in Zimbabwe. Zimbabwe is of interest for several reasons. First and most basic, Zimbabwe is one of relatively few sub-Saharan African countries with an established corporate sector and a company accounts database which is long-established and of good quality, as we discuss below. Zimbabwe was included in the sample of countries originally considered by Singh and Hamid (1992) and by BADM (2001), and further results for Zimbabwe therefore offer an interesting perspective on previous research. Second, the Zimbabwean corporate sector has evolved through three major and dramatically-different economic regimes: the Unilateral Declaration of Independence (UDI) period (1965-1979), the first decade of independence (1980-1990) and the Economic Structural Adjustment Programme (ESAP) period that started in December 1991. During the UDI period, international sanctions were imposed on Zimbabwe, forcing the government to adopt an import substitution industrialisation policy. At that time, the only source of external finance for the corporate sector was the domestic financial system. During the first decade of independence the economy was heavily controlled and by the late 1980s there were serious problems of high unemployment levels, inflation rates and a growing budget deficit. As an attempt to address these economic problems, the government adopted an economic reform programme in 1991 with the aim of raising savings, investment and economic growth.[1] Thus Zimbabwe has evolved through three very different economic policy regimes and it offers a particularly interesting setting within which to examine questions about economic policy, financial sector growth and company financial behaviour.

In this study we concentrate on evaluating the impact of the economic reform programme begun in 1991. We set up an eclectic but orthodox model of capital structure to test hypotheses about the financing decisions of listed firms in Zimbabwe. We then enlarge this model to include factors which model the possible effects of the economic reform programme. Among these factors we distinguish between the direct channels of policy such as tax rate changes and indirect channels such as improvements in the capital market which flow from broad measures of financial sector reform. Our main hypothesis is that economic reform has helped make financial decisions more transparent and has improved the financing opportunities of the corporate sector in Zimbabwe.

The rest of the paper is organized as follows. Section 2 describes the basic facts about corporate financing in Zimbabwe over the period 1990-99. Section 3 summarizes the main theories of capital structure and sets out the model to be tested. Section 4 contains the results of estimating this model and evaluates the impact of economic reform. Summary and conclusions are presented in Section 5.

THE PATTERN OF CORPORATE FINANCING IN ZIMBABWE

In this section, we summarise the patterns of corporate financing in Zimbabwe using company accounts data. The main objective of the analysis is to investigate the role of the domestic financial markets, particularly banks and the stock market in financing the Zimbabwean corporate sector in the period 1990-99, just prior to and then following economic reform. The data consist of the annual accounts of 52 non-financial companies listed on the Zimbabwe Stock Exchange from its inception in 1946 through 1999, but excluding companies that were either delisted or taken over. The data were obtained from the annual reports of the individual companies and from various issues of the Zimbabwe Stock Exchange Handbook.[2]

Table 1 shows the gross sources of finance for the 52 sample companies for the period under review. These data were calculated by summing the cash amounts from each source over all companies and then expressing the totals as percentages of gross investment. For 1990-99 as a whole (the rightmost column), the cash amounts were summed over time and then expressed as percentages of the total for 1990-99. This methodology for measuring corporate financial structures is most nearly akin to that proposed by Corbett and Jenkinson (1997) and used by Cobham and Subramaniam (1998) in their study of India.

Since the basic financing choice faced by firms is between internal and external sources, we subdivided the sources accordingly. Internal sources were further subdivided into depreciation and retained profits. External sources were subdivided into long-term and short-term. Long-term finance comprises equity, bonds, bank loans, foreign loans, finance lease, hire purchase, and others. Equity finance is mainly composed of

TABLE 1. Zimbabwe: Listed Companies' Gross Sources of Finance, 1990-99 (52 Companies; in Per-Cent of Total Financing)

	1990	1991	1992	1993	1994	1995	1996	1997	1998	1999	1990-99
Internal Finance	16.3	17.8	17.7	19.7	28.7	22.9	19.9	17.9	25.3	32.8	24.6
Retained Income	9.4	12.0	10.9	12.9	22.0	14.1	12.0	10.9	18.5	25.8	17.5
Depreciation	6.9	5.8	6.8	6.7	6.7	8.8	7.9	7.0	6.9	7.0	7.1
External Finance	83.7	82.2	82.3	80.3	71.3	77.1	80.1	82.1	74.7	67.2	75.4
Long-term Finance	29.8	37.4	32.0	26.4	24.9	29.3	30.8	34.6	15.4	14.9	23.6
Equity Finance	8.8	17.6	6.4	7.9	7.0	7.6	9.5	20.5	2.7	2.8	7.8
Bonds	0.9	2.7	1.0	0.2	0.2	1.6	0.7	1.8	1.1	0.7	1.0
Bank Loans	2.6	2.0	1.3	2.1	0.9	0.3	1.7	1.8	1.1	0.5	1.2
Foreign Loans	3.0	2.7	2.1	3.2	11.9	10.3	8.9	4.7	2.0	3.8	5.0
Finance Lease	0	0	0	0	0	1.3	1.0	0.4	2.4	0.4	0.9
Hire Purchase	0.1	0	0	0	0	0	1.0	0	2.0	0.3	0.6
Other sources	14.4	12.4	21.2	12.9	4.8	8.2	7.9	5.3	4.1	6.3	7.2
Short-term Finance	53.9	44.8	50.3	54.0	46.4	47.8	49.3	47.6	59.3	52.3	51.8
Bank Overdraft	8.5	8.6	14.7	8.8	8.8	8.7	6.2	7.4	11.5	9.5	9.3
Bank Acceptance	2.6	1.3	1.7	2.6	2.2	1.2	3.2	2.7	4.1	1.3	2.4
Trade Credit	27.3	18.5	24.1	27.1	22.7	23.7	25.7	23.9	35.5	29.3	27.8
Other S/Term Sources	15.4	16.4	9.8	15.5	12.7	14.3	14.2	13.6	8.2	12.2	12.2

new and rights issues. Bonds consist of preference shares and debentures. Bank loans represent medium and long-term loans provided by the domestic banking sector, mainly commercial banks and the Zimbabwe Development Bank. Foreign loans encompass offshore financing and other foreign loans from institutions such as the International Finance Corporation and the African Development Bank. 'Other' long-term sources consist of loans from domestic non-bank financial institutions, such as pension funds and building societies. Short-term finance comprises bank overdrafts, bank acceptances, trade credit and other short-term sources. 'Other' short-term sources consist of the portion of long-term debt falling due in a year's time and other short-term borrowings not included in the other categories.

For 1990-99 as a whole, external finance contributed 75% of total funds and internal finance provided the remaining 25%. Short-term finance accounted for 52% of external funds with long-term finance contributing the remaining 23%. There were some interesting differences among the different components of *long-term finance*. Equity financing was the most important source of long-term finance at 8%. 'Other' sources of long-term finance (7%) were the second most important source, and foreign loans contributed 5% of external funds. Long-term bank loans and bonds were each a very minor component of total external financing. The most important source of *short-term* financing was from trade credit, which provided about 29% of the total, with most of the remaining 23% being provided by banks. Table 1 shows that there were surges in equity financing in 1991 and 1997 when equities contributed as much as 18% and 21% (respectively) of total financing. The high contribution of the stock market in these years may be related to policy changes involving the raising of barriers to foreign investors. These changes took place in 1991 at the start of the overall economic reform program, and at the end of 1996 when entry barriers to foreign investors were lowered further. Clearly though, the data suggest that the increased use of the equity market which followed these reforms was very short-lived, a phenomenon that was also documented for India in the 1980s by Cobham and Subramaniam (1998). However, GMS argued that increased use of the equity market in India in the 1990s was more long-lived.

It is interesting to compare the results from our study with other comparable studies. Singh and Hamid (1992) and Singh (1995) examined the financing patterns in Zimbabwe for the period 1980-89.[3] Exceptionally among the countries they study, their data suggest that *internal* finance was more important than external finance in Zimbabwe. Our results suggest that Zimbabwean companies relied more heavily on *exter-*

nal finance and are therefore more consistent with the other countries studied by Singh and Hamid. The difference between our findings and those of Singh and Hamid are more likely to be due to the different time periods studied than to the different methodologies used, as the Singh method tends to produce a *higher* share of external financing than ours. Singh and Hamid's data covers the early independence period following the end of UDI when Zimbabwean companies were largely forced to rely on their own resources, whereas our data covers a later period when the economy was more open. This would be consistent with the higher share of external financing that we find. Singh (1995) also reported a much higher share of equity finance in Zimbabwe (43.5%) than we do (8%). This difference probably is due more to methodological differences, as Singh's method does tend to produce a higher share of equity financing than ours. See *inter alia* Cobham and Subramaniam (1998) on these methodological points.

A MODEL OF CAPITAL STRUCTURE DECISIONS

The theory of capital structure has been comprehensively reviewed in several recent papers. Examples include Harris and Raviv (1991) who concentrate primarily on theoretical issues and Prasad, Green, and Murinde (2001), who focus on applications in developing countries. For this reason we do not attempt a comprehensive literature survey in this section. Instead, Table 2 summarizes the main variables suggested by theory which are usually thought to influence a company's capital structure. These variables are derived from four of the main strands of literature which can be summarised as follows. First are theories based on asymmetric information as between different stakeholders in the firm, a seminal contribution in this strand being Myers' (1984) pecking order theory; second are agency theories, notably Jensen and Meckling (1976); third are transactions costs theories of the firm, advocated particularly by Williamson (1988); and fourth are extensions of Modigliani and Miller (1963) which argue that differential taxation of corporations and their stakeholders set up incentives for firms to finance their activities in particular ways.

Table 3 summarizes the main empirical studies with a bearing on the application of these variables in modelling capital structure. The list of references is intended to be illustrative and certainly not comprehensive. Table 3 includes the same firm-specific variables as Table 2. However, it should be emphasized that the corporate tax rate is both a

TABLE 2. Theoretical Determinants of Debt Ratios

Firm Factor	Impact on Leverage	Reason	Model	Reference
Profitability	Positive	Pecking order hypothesis	Asymmetric information	Myers (1984)
	Negative	Enhances firm's ability to borrow		
Size	Positive	Less vulnerable to bank-ruptcy	Asymmetric information	Myers (1984)
Free Cash Flow	Positive	Pre-commitment	Agency	Jensen(1986)
Growth opportunities	Negative	Under-investment problem	Agency	Myers (1977)
Asset Tangibility	Positive	Collaterals	Agency	Jensen and Meckling (1976)
	Positive	Reduces bankruptcy costs	Transaction costs	Williamson (1988)
Risk	Negative	Bankruptcy costs	Transaction costs	Myers (1977)
Corporate tax rate	Positive	Reduces corporate tax burden	Taxation	Modgliani & Miller (1963)
Non-debt tax shields	Negative	Shields firm tax	Taxation	DeAngelo & Masulis (1980)
Asset diversification	Positive	Reduces risk		

TABLE 3. Summary of Empirical Studies

Factor	Expected Sign	Theoretical Reference	Empirical Evidence Positive	Negative
Profitability	Positive Negative	Rajan & Zingales (1995) Myers (1984)		Titman & Wissels (1988) Jensen & Meckling (1992)
Size	Positive	Kim & Sorensen (1986)	Firth (1995) Hussain (1997)	Titman & Wissels (1988)
Free cash flow	Positive	Jensen (1986)	Shenoy and Koch (1996)	Lowe, Naughton, & Taylor (1994)
Growth opportunities	Negative	Myers (1977) Jensen (1986)	Krishnan & Moyer (1996)	Homaifar, Zietz & Benkato (1994)
Asset tangibility	Positive	Myers (1977)	Jensen & Meckling (1992) Thies & Klock (1992)	
Risk	Negative	Bradley, Jarrell & Kim (1984)		Mackie-Mason (1990) Saa-Requejo (1996)
Corporate tax rate	Positive	Modgliani and Miller (1963)	Homaifar, Zietz & Benkato (1994)	Krishnan & Moyer (1996)
Non-debt tax shields	Negative	DeAngelo & Masulis (1980)	Boyle & Eckhold (1997)	Wiwattanakantang (1999)
Inflation	Positive	BADM (2001)		BADM (2001)
Bank liquidity	Positive	Demirguc-Kunt & Maksimovic (1996)	BADM (2001)	
Stock market development	Negative	Demirguc-Kunt & Maksimovic (1996)		BADM (2001)

BADM: Booth, Aivazian, Demirguc-Kunt, & Maksimovic (2001)

firm-specific variable, depending as it does on each firm's financial position in relation to deductibles such as depreciation, and a policy channel as it also depends on the corporate tax rules in place at any given time. Table 3 includes a further set of 3 macro-economic variables: measures of inflation, bank liquidity, and stock market development. These variables are policy- and development-related variables which model the impact of financial development and financial reform on firm behaviour. See BADM (2001) for details. These variables are an important component of our effort to model and understand the impact of the policy reform process in Zimbabwe.

Even the brief summary contained in Table 3 underlines the conclusion of Prasad, Green and Murinde (2001) that the empirical literature on corporate capital structure is relatively fragmented. Notwithstanding some of the main theoretical predictions, it is not difficult to obtain a variety of empirical results, some of which are consistent with one or another underlying theory and others which are not consistent with any current theory. In this paper we do not seek to make a new contribution to capital structure theory. Rather we aim to use an eclectic model as a vehicle for arriving at a preliminary evaluation of the impact of economic policy reforms on capital structure decisions. The general empirical model which we estimate can be written using standard notation as:

$$Y_{jt} = \sum_i \beta_i X_{ijt} + \varepsilon_{jt}$$

Here, Y_{jt} is the capital structure measure which we seek to explain, X_{ijt} are $i = 1, \ldots, I$ explanatory variables, and $j = 1, \ldots, J$ indexes the firms in the sample. The empirical counterparts to these variables are described next.

Y_{jt} = The debt ratio, defined as the ratio of total debt to total assets. This variable can be defined in many different ways. See *inter alia* Rajan and Zingales (1995) and Green, Murinde and Suppakitjarak (2001). It transpires that the general character of our results are not affected by the definition which is chosen. Therefore, to avoid excessive repetition, we only present results for total debt/total assets, as this is the statistic which is most straightforward to compute on a broadly comparable basis across countries. See Mutenheri (2001) for further details.

The explanatory variables and the expected signs of their coefficients are given as follows:

Profitability $(-/+)$ = ratio of operating income to total assets.
Size $(+)$ = log of total assets.

Cash flow (+) = income attributable to shareholders as a proportion of turnover.

Dividends (−) = dividend payable as a proportion of operating income. This is included as a supplementary indicator of firm liquidity. Following Shenoy and Koch (1996) we assume that dividends are predetermined in relation to the capital structure decision.

Growth opportunities (−) = percentage change in total assets.

Asset tangibility (+) = ratio of fixed assets to total assets.

Risk (−) = ratio of unexpected income to total assets. Unexpected income is estimated as the absolute values of the residuals from firm-specific regressions of net income before interest and tax on a constant and a time trend.

Corporate tax rate (+) = the ratio of tax paid to operating income.

Inflation (+) = percentage change in consumer price index, an (inverse) measure of real financing costs.

Bank liquidity (+) = the ratio of M2 to GDP, a proxy for bank development.

Stock market development (+) = the ratio of stock market capitalisation to GDP, a proxy for stock market development.

Data for the estimation of the model was collected from the financial statements of 18 companies listed on the Zimbabwe Stock Exchange from 1985 to 1999. The dataset was then divided into two sub-samples. The first subsample covers 1986-1990, the period of financial repression and this is referred to as equation 1 in the following discussion. Equation 2 covers 1995-1999, corresponding to the post-reform period. Given that reform began in 1991, it was decided to omit the years 1991-94 on the grounds that the impact of reform would be felt only gradually. By 1995, the reforms were mostly in place and firms would have had time to adjust to them and complete a transition to a new equilibrium. We took the view that the sample was too small and the possible adjustments too complex for it to be useful for us to attempt the estimation of a dynamic model to study the transition process itself. However, for completeness we did also estimate a third equation using data from the entire sample period 1986-1999. The model was estimated using both the fixed effects and random effects methods. F tests were used to test for the validity of the fixed effects against the null of pooled OLS, and Hausman tests were used to compare the fixed effects and random effects methods. See for example Baltagi (1995) for details.

EMPIRICAL RESULTS

The results from the three regression equations and the relevant diagnostics are presented in Table 4. Individual effects are important in all 3 equations. However, the Hausman tests suggest that the random effects method is an adequate parameterisation of equations 1 and 3, whereas the fixed effects method is required for equation 2.

It is evident that there are substantial differences between the estimated equations for the pre-reform and post-reform periods. In the pre-reform period, 5 out of 11 variables have the theoretically expected sign, and only one variable (asset tangibility) is significant. Moreover, the sign of the coefficient on tangibility ($-$) would suggest that firms with more fixed assets tend to borrow less, which is not consistent with the predictions of theory, as suggested by Jensen and Meckling (1976) or Williamson (1988). A possible explanation for this relationship is that the variable may be a proxy for the non-debt tax shields of Zimbabwean firms rather than a measure of asset specificity. In Zimbabwe, a wide range of fixed assets qualify for a Special Initial Allowance which allows 100% first year depreciation of fixed assets for corporate tax purposes. Companies that acquired fixed assets enjoy a substantial tax shelter, which in turn would reduce the taxable income that could be shielded by debt. Thus, purchases of fixed assets may tend to dominate the tangibility ratio and also the tax shields enjoyed by Zimbabwean firms. Comparing our results for equation 1 with those of BADM, who estimated equations for the total debt ratio for Zimbabwe covering 1980-90, we find a rather broad similarity in that they too find few significant coefficients[4] and many counter-intuitive signs, such as a negative coefficient on firm size. However, their analysis ends in 1990 before the reform programme got under way.

The results from equation 2 show that 6 variables have the theoretically expected sign and 5 variables have significant coefficients. Asset tangibility is now positively related to the debt ratio and significant at the 10% level suggesting that during the post-reform period firms with collateral assets might have better access to the debt market. The change of sign of the tangibility ratio would suggest that during the first decade of independence, access to the debt market was determined by factors not captured by the included variables, whereas after the implementation of the reform program, access to the debt market required collateral assets. The demand for collateral by banks in the post-reform era was such that it led to the establishment of the Venture Capital Company of Zimbabwe and the Indigenous Business Development Centre in order

TABLE 4. Regression Results

Explanatory variable	Expected sign	Pre-reform (1986-90) Random Effects	Post-reform (1995-99) Fixed Effects	Pooled (1986-99) Random Effects
Profitability	$-/+$	0.038	0.238	-0.046
		(0.290)	(1.433)	(0.755)
Size	$+$	2.911	5.450	3.595
		(0.463)	(0.803)	(2.493)**
Cash flow	$+$	-0.028	-0.300	-0.027
		(0.423)	(1.177)	(0.585)
Dividends	$-$	0.074	-0.045	-0.015
		(1.337)	(0.451)	(0.423)
Growth opportunities	$-$	0.010	0.065	-0.005
		(0.256)	(1.888)*	(0.263)
Asset tangibility	$+$	-0.202	0.234	0.032
		(2.305)**	(1.884)*	(0.682)
Firm risk	$-$	-0.012	0.242	0.066
		(0.207)	(2.578)***	(2.146)**
Corporate tax rate	$+$	-0.034	-0.294	-0.027
		(0.639)	(3.322)***	(0.854)
Inflation	$+$	0.247	-0.100	-0.029
		(0.622)	(1.047)	(0.530)
Bank liquidity	$+$	-1.953	0.964	0.488
		(0.552)	(2.795)***	(2.378)**
Stock market	$-$	-0.217	-0.004	-0.010
		(1.079)	(0.059)	(0.220)
Specification Tests				
Test for company effects		$F(17,61) = 15.7$	$F(17,61) = 5.0$	$F(17,151) = 5.5$
Hausman test		$\chi^2(11) = 8.9$	$\chi^2(11) = 20.9$	$\chi^2(11) = 16.1$

Notes
T statistics are in parentheses. Significance shown by: * 10%, level; ** 5% level; *** 1% level
Critical values at 5% level for: $F(17,61) = 1.84$; $F(17,151) = 1.67$; $\chi^2(11) = 19.7$

to cater for the financing needs of small- and medium-scale enterprises. This clearly suggests how the reform programme did alter firm behaviour. The other variable which is significant at the 10% level, is the growth rate which is positively related to firm debt ratios, suggesting that firms with high growth rates use more debt than those with low growth rates. This is contrary to orthodox theory but may be reasonable in the Zimbabwean context. Outsiders in a thin equity market may have more difficulty in recognising a firm's growth opportunities than would more specialized outsiders in banks, leading to a preference of growth-oriented firms for more debt.

The tax rate, firm risk and bank liquidity are all significant at the 1% level, although the first two of these coefficients have counter-theoretical signs. The negative relation between the tax rate and the debt ratio is still consistent with the findings of Krishnan and Moyer (1996) among others. In Zimbabwe, the relationship could be attributable to an expectational effect induced by government tax policy. The corporate tax rate was reduced every year from 1980 to 1999. Companies would therefore have had an incentive to bring forward tax shelters as much as possible to maximise their tax benefits prior to the next cut. Thus, successive tax cuts would be associated with increases in debt ratios as firms expected further tax cuts in the future. The positive coefficient on firm risk could be explained by the fact that firms with risky earnings seek external funds (working capital) to smooth their financing. This is especially plausible in Zimbabwe where we noted in section 3 that on average short-term loans constituted about 52% of firms' external finance. This is consistent with Myers' (1977) argument that short-term debt may be positively related to risk. This result implies that banks play an important role in providing short-term loans to listed firms. The positive coefficient on bank liquidity suggests that the development of banks encourages corporate borrowing. It is particularly striking that this coefficient changes sign between the pre-reform and post-reform periods.

In the third equation, seven coefficients have the correct sign and three are significant. However, given the differences between equations 1 and 2 we do not attach much importance to the pooled estimates as a stable 'model' of the whole period.

Overall, the results from the three equations suggest that the conventional theory of capital structure has relatively little explanatory power in the pre-reform period in the sense that only one variable is significant in the debt equation in the pre-reform period whereas five variables are significant in the post-reform era. Economic regulations by the government in the first decade of independence constrained company financing behaviour. It could mean that during this period, firms were operating at sub-optimal debt ratios implying an inefficient allocation of resources. The structural adjustment programme appears to have changed this behaviour to some extent. Firm size, asset tangibility, tax rates, cash flow, earnings volatility and bank liquidity became important determinants of corporate capital structures in the post-reform era. However, the results from the second equation seem to suggest that firms with high growth rates and fluctuating earnings borrowed more than those with low growth rates and stable earnings, suggesting that the orthodox theories of capital structure may need modification in the context of developing countries like Zimbabwe. Moreover, the results from equation 2 show that profitability, dividends, cash flow, stock market development, and inflation are not significant determinants of corporate financing decisions. This suggests that although the structural adjustment program may have addressed some of the economic problems in Zimbabwe, more still needs to be done and this might explain why company behaviour does not respond to some of the factors suggested in the literature to be of importance for capital structure decisions.

SUMMARY AND CONCLUSIONS

In this paper, we first empirically examined the financing pattern of the Zimbabwean corporate sector, using company accounts data. Our major conclusion from this examination is that listed firms rely heavily on external finance, especially short-term bank financing. Long-term bank loans make little contribution to financing of the corporate sector. The stock market, on the other hand, does seem to contribute significantly to the financing of the corporate sector. Second, we econometrically investigated key determinants of firms' financial behaviour suggested by the theory of finance, but augmented by variables aimed at capturing the impact of economic reforms and financial development in Zimbabwe. Our main conclusion from this analysis is that these factors have limited power to explain the capital structure of listed firms during the pre-reform period. However in the post-reform period, asset tangibility, tax rates, growth opportunities, earnings volatility and bank liquidity are all significant determinants of capital structure. The differences between the pre-reform and post-reform era suggest that the reforms did achieve a partial success in opening up the capital markets and improving the transparency of firm financing behaviour.

NOTES

1. Details of the reform programme are given in Mutenheri (2001).
2. Data on equity issues were kindly provided by Oliver Lutz of Sagit stockbrokers.
3. BADM (2001) used balance sheet data in their study of Zimbabwe and other developing countries, and their statistics are therefore not strictly comparable with ours.

In particular, it is difficult to derive information on internal and external financing from balance sheet data. Green, Murinde and Suppakitjarak (2001) discuss this point.

4. BADM's results are hard to interpret because they report fixed and random effects estimates but do not provide any basic diagnostics such as Hausman tests.

REFERENCES

Baltagi, B.H., 1995, *Econometric analysis of panel data*, New York, Wiley.

Booth, L., Aivazian, V., Demirguc-Kunt, A., Maksimovic, V. 2001, "Capital structures in developing countries," *Journal of Finance*, Vol. 56, No. 1, pp. 87-130.

Boyle, G.W., and Eckhold, K.R., 1997, "Capital structure choice and financial market liberalisation: Evidence from New Zealand," *Applied Financial Economic*, Vol. 7, pp. 427-437.

Bradley, M., Jarrell, G. and Kim, E.H., 1984, "On the existence of an optimal capital structure: theory and evidence," *Journal of Finance*, Vol. 39, pp. 857-878.

Cobham, D. and Subramaniam, R., 1998, "Corporate finance in developing countries: new evidence for India," *World Development*, Vol. 26, No. 6, pp. 1033-1047.

Corbett, J. and Jenkinson, T., 1997, "How is investment financed? A study of Germany, Japan, the United Kingdom and the United States," *Manchester School*, Vol. 65, Supplement, pp. 69-93.

DeAngelo, H. and Masulis, R.W., 1980, "Optimal capital structure under corporate and personal taxation," *Journal of Financial Economics*, Vol. 8, pp. 3-29.

Demirguc-Kunt, A. and Maksimovic, V., 1996, "Stock market development and financing choices of firms," *The World Bank Economic Review*, Vol. 10, pp. 341-369.

Firth, M., 1995, "The impact of institutional stockholders and managerial interests on the capital structure of firms," *Managerial and Decision Economics*, Vol.16, pp. 167-175.

Green, C.J., Murinde, V. and Suppakitjarak, J., 2001, "Corporate financial structures in India," *Finance and Development Research Programme Working Paper*, forthcoming.

Harris, M. and Raviv, A., 1991, "The theory of capital structure," *Journal of Finance*, Vol. 49, pp. 297-355.

Homaifar, G., Zietz, J., and Benkato, O., 1994, "An empirical model of capital structure, some new evidence," *Journal of Business Finance and Accounting*, Vol. 21, pp. 1-14.

Jensen, M.C. 1986, "Agency Costs of Free Cash Flow, Corporate Finance and Take-overs," *American Economic Review*, Vol. 76, pp. 323-339.

Jensen, M.C. and Meckling, W.H., 1976, "Theory of the firm: Managerial behaviour, agency costs and ownership structure," *Journal of Financial Economics*, Vol. 3, pp. 305-360.

Jensen, M.C. and Meckling, W.H., 1992, "Specific and General Knowledge, and Organizational Structure," in L. Werin and H. Wijkander (eds.), *Contract Economics*, Massachusetts, Blackwell.

Kim, W.S. and Sorensen, E.H., 1986, "Evidence on the Impact of the Agency Costs of Debt in Corporate Debt Policy," *Journal of Financial and Quantitative Analysis,* Vol. 21, pp. 131-144.

Krishnan,V.S. and Moyer, R.C., 1996, "Determinants of capital structure: An empirical analysis of firms in industrialised countries," *Managerial Finance,* Vol. 22, pp. 39-55.

Lowe, J., Naughton, T. and Taylor, P., 1994, "The Impact of Corporate Strategy on the Capital Structure of Australian Companies," *Managerial and Decision Economics,* Vol. 15, pp. 245-257.

Mackie-Mason, J. 1990, "Do Firms Care Who Provides Their Financing?", in R. G. Hubbard (ed.), *Asymmetric Information, Corporate Finance and Investment,* Chicago and London: University of Chicago Press.

Mayer, C., 1988, "New issues in corporate finance," *European Economic Review,* Vol. 32, pp. 1167-1189.

Modigliani, F. and Miller, M.H., 1963, "Corporate income taxes and the cost of capital: A correction," *American Economic Review,* Vol. 53, pp. 433-443.

Mutenheri, E., 2001, "Financing decisions of listed firms in Zimbabwe," *mimeo.*

Myers, S.C., 1977, "Determinants of corporate borrowing," *Journal of Financial Economics,* Vol. 5, pp. 147-175.

Myers, S.C., 1984, "The capital structure puzzle," *Journal of Finance,* Vol. 34, pp. 575-592.

Prasad, S., Green, C.J., and Murinde, V., 2001, "Company financing, capital structure, and ownership," *SUERF Study* No 12, Vienna, SUERF.

Rajan, R. and Zingales, L., 1995, "What do we know about capital structure? Some evidence from international data," *Journal of Finance,* Vol. 50, pp. 1421-1460.

Saa-Requejo, J., 1996, "Financing decisions: Lessons from the Spanish experience," Vol. 25, pp. 44-56.

Shenoy, C. and Koch, P.D., 1996, "The firm's leverage-cash flow relationship," *Journal of Empirical Finance,* Vol. 2, pp. 307-331.

Singh, A., 1995, "Corporate financial patterns in industrialising economies: a comparative study," *IFC Technical Paper No. 2,* Washington D.C., International Finance Corporation.

Singh, A. and Hamid, J., 1992, "Corporate financial structures in developing countries," *IFC Technical Paper No. 1,* Washington D.C., International Finance Corporation.

Thies, C.F. and Klock, M.S., 1992, "Determinants of Capital Structure," *Review of Financial Economics,* Vol. 1, pp. 40-52.

Titman, S. and Wessels, R., 1988, "The determinants of capital structure choice," *Journal of Finance,* Vol. 43, pp. 1-19.

Williamson, O.E., 1988, "Corporate finance and corporate governance," *Journal of Finance,* Vol. 43, pp. 567-591.

Wiwattanakantang, Y., 1999, "An Empirical study on the determinants of the structure of Thai Firms," *Pacific-basin Finance Journal,* Vol. 7, pp. 371-403.

Index